Commuters' Book Exchange
2011-2012
Convenor: Marion Toms 542 2917
Please pass this book on or before

Oct. 11	to	Jane Anema
Nov.1	to	Jo Saunders
Nov.22	to	Diane Esplen
Dec.13	to	Gerry Kinahan
Jan.10	to	Mary Marshall
Jan.31	to	Fay Pole
Feb.21	to	Marion Toms
Mar.20	to	Judie Scott
Apr.10	to	Joyce Hoffman

The
Last
Rain

EDEET RAVEL

VIKING
CANADA

VIKING CANADA

Published by the Penguin Group

Penguin Group (Canada), 90 Eglinton Avenue East, Suite 700,
Toronto, Ontario, Canada M4P 2Y3 (a division of Pearson Canada Inc.)

Penguin Group (USA) Inc., 375 Hudson Street, New York, New York 10014, U.S.A.
Penguin Books Ltd, 80 Strand, London WC2R 0RL, England
Penguin Ireland, 25 St Stephen's Green, Dublin 2, Ireland
(a division of Penguin Books Ltd)
Penguin Group (Australia), 250 Camberwell Road, Camberwell,
Victoria 3124, Australia (a division of Pearson Australia Group Pty Ltd)
Penguin Books India Pvt Ltd, 11 Community Centre,
Panchsheel Park, New Delhi – 110 017, India
Penguin Group (NZ), 67 Apollo Drive, Rosedale, North Shore 0745,
Auckland, New Zealand (a division of Pearson New Zealand Ltd)
Penguin Books (South Africa) (Pty) Ltd, 24 Sturdee Avenue,
Rosebank, Johannesburg 2196, South Africa

Penguin Books Ltd, Registered Offices: 80 Strand, London WC2R 0RL, England

First published 2011

1 2 3 4 5 6 7 8 9 10 (RRD)

Manufactured in the U.S.A.

LIBRARY AND ARCHIVES CANADA CATALOGUING IN PUBLICATION

Ravel, Edeet, 1955–
The last rain / Edeet Ravel.

ISBN 978-0-670-06866-1

I. Title.

PS8585.A8715L38 2011   C813'.54   C2011-900749-5

Visit the Penguin Group (Canada) website at **www.penguin.ca**

Special and corporate bulk purchase rates available;
please see **www.penguin.ca/corporatesales** or call 1-800-810-3104, ext. 2477 or 2474

for my sister Sara

Author's Note

I began working on this story thirty-five years ago, when I was twenty. Written in the voice of a young girl, it was based on my childhood at Kibbutz Sasa in the northern Galilee, with an eighteen-month interlude in Montreal. I felt wrenched from my home when my parents left the kibbutz for good; I had just turned seven and for the next few years I daydreamed continually about returning. I never did return.

The subject of this backward look has remained consistent over the years, but changing perceptions have no doubt affected the child's voice. I have also added to her account stray sections of what the poet Carl Sandburg called the labyrinth of sliding doors that is our collective past. Because no analogy can capture with finality what is never final, Sandburg contemplates another image: a book of ciphers, with its code buried inside a cave in the Sargasso Sea. The only way I can think of to explore that labyrinth, those ciphers, is through fiction.

I have capitalized several terms that take on special meaning in kibbutz culture: Children's House, Group, Minder, Room, Dining Hall, Kitchen, Guard, Pioneer, Hike, Wake-Up, Bedding-Down. The First Rain and the Last Rain have proper names in Hebrew—*yoreh* and *malkosh*.

In past centuries, literary works were dedicated to kings and queens. You, readers, are today's royalty; may my efforts please you.

Dramatis Personae

Eldar Members (selected)

The Satie Family
Naftali Satie ("Nat"/"Ricky")
Varda Klein Satie ("Avra"/"Rita")
David Satie (b 1950)
Dori Satie (b 1955)
Sara Satie (b 1959)

Dori's Group
Lulu
Skye
Gilead
Simon
Elan
Jonathan
Hannah

David's Group
Noam
Amnoni
Hagar

Founders
Martin Dubrovsky ("Michael")
Isaac Milman ("Eli"?/"Rubin"?)
Edna
Amos
Dafna
Lou
Coco
Nina

Israeli-born Contingent
Shoshana, Ora, Yael, Emanuel,
Katzi, Tamir, Oded

Thane
Jeremiah Ben-Jacob

Timeline

June 1955 to June 1959	*Eldar*
June 1959 to December 1960	*Canada*
January 1961 to June 1962	*Eldar*

I

Utopia

Utopia. From Gr. not (οὐ) + place
(τόπος), i.e., no-place; an imaginary
island, depicted by Sir Thomas More
(1516) as a perfect social, legal and
political system.

—OXFORD ENGLISH DICTIONARY

Daily Schedule for Kindergarten/ Transitional First Grade Eldar, 1960

Wake-Up (Minder)

dress, wash up, free play

breakfast

directed play with teacher[1]
(art, stories, singing, holidays, nature, Hikes, literacy, numbers)

mid-morning snack

directed play

lunch

shower (if required)

two-hour nap

Wake-Up (on-duty monitor)

snack

three-hour visit with parents

return to Children's House

supper

shower, pyjamas

Bedding-Down

Dori

We'll build our country our country our homeland
Because this country belongs to us
We'll build our country our country our homeland
Something blood something something generations
In spite of those who set out to destroy us
Fire something freedom something hope

I never can catch all the words.

Our First Year

On a cold day in January 1949, a small group of American Jews from the Young Guard Youth Movement unloaded their beds, straw mattresses, and toothbrushes, planted themselves in a deserted Arab village near the Lebanese border of Israel, and called themselves Kibbutz[2] Eldar. The fact was registered in the Zionist press throughout the world, in small or large paragraphs, depending on the source, and was then probably forgotten, as most news is.[3]

Dori

I'm on the sofa in my parents' Room. At night their sofa opens into a bed.

I could sleep on the floor next to them. I wouldn't mind sleeping on the stone tiles in my clothes. I wouldn't even need a blanket.

But Daddy says *time to go back to the Children's House sweetie.*

Those words fly straight to my stomach. The Children's House is as far away as the stars in the sky.

Pinocchio

Once upon a time, many centuries ago, there was—

"A king!" my little readers will say immediately.

No, children, you are mistaken. Once upon a time there was a piece of wood.

Dori

Unfortunately children aren't allowed to sleep in the Rooms. We're free but not that free.

I could pretend to fall asleep. That way Daddy will have to carry me back. Or I could beg for another page of *Pinocchio.*

Or I could do both. First beg for another page and then pretend to fall asleep.

Daddy believes that with children you have to say yes. That's lucky for me. Very lucky. Not all children are so lucky. I beg for another page and he agrees. I told you!

Daddy was away for three months. He wasn't here when it snowed. I didn't want to play in the snow because nothing counted until he came back. Besides there was snow in Canada—though I must say I prefer the snow in

4

Eldar. It makes a very loud noise when you walk on it and you can smell it on the earth and on the leaves. The snow in Canada didn't have a smell.

I waited for Daddy the whole time he was away. I don't know why he had to stay in Canada but he promised to come back and he did.

Parents aren't allowed to break a promise.

Snow Boycott

Dori

Mostly I like *Pinocchio*. I don't understand some parts. I don't understand the part with the cricket and I don't really know what a cricket is. If I was the writer I'd choose a butterfly or a lizard. Lizards sleep on rocks in the sun and if you're very quiet you can touch their soft skin before they run away.

I don't understand the part with the non-Jewish wig[4] either. What is that all about?

Israelis wear non-Jewish wigs too by the way. Not Pioneers of course. But Israelis in cities for example. I don't know why it's called a non-Jewish wig.

I love the fairy with the blue hair. She's so beautiful!

Daddy says *now we really have to go—it's very late.* There's nothing I can do. I asked for another page of *Pinocchio* and Daddy read me another page. And now we have to go back.

I have to decide. If I pretend to fall asleep Daddy will carry me but if we walk I can walk very slowly.

Daddy takes my hand and we leave the Room. In the evening the plants and bushes have a marvellous smell. The darker it gets the more marvellous the smell gets. The sun is starting to set but it's not dark yet. Soon the Last Rain will fall. We won't know for sure it's the Last Rain until it doesn't rain again. If it doesn't rain again we'll look back and say *that was the Last Rain.*

Unless the Last Rain comes very late. If it comes after a long time without rain then we'll know for sure that it's the Last Rain.

Rooms[5]

Dori

People say the mountains are beautiful but I don't know why. The mountains are never an interesting colour. They're always dark brown or dark grey or dark green. There's nothing beautiful about them.

Everyone is excited because you can see Mount Hermon from Eldar. I'm the only one who can't see it. I can't see it and I don't know why it's exciting but I'm also excited.

Behind the mountains lies the Enemy. Unfortunately the Enemy wants to destroy us. The Enemy keeps trying and we keep fighting back. It isn't easy but so far we're succeeding.

My brother David says the country behind the mountains is Syria but his friend Noam says it's Lebanon. David says Syria hates us more than Lebanon but Noam says they both hate us the same.

Our First Year

13 January 1949. The process of settlement took place so suddenly that most of us haven't had enough time to digest its significance.

We were told to expect settlement within a short time.

We were told to consider Eldar, an Arab village none of us had ever heard of before, in the high and windy hills of Galilee.

We were told to prepare to leave our interim kibbutz in five days.

We packed our stuff into three trucks, rode to the North, unloaded, and started on the life-long process of building a new community in the Palestinian wilderness.

From Los Angeles, Chicago, New York and other points, to Eldar. Indescribably exciting and almost unbelievable.

Dori

Well here we are. Here we are. We're late but Shoshana doesn't mind. That's because of Daddy. Shoshana knows that if she does anything to me I'll tell Daddy and he'll get angry. That's why I'm safe. Jonathan and Skye are safe too.

Daddy is laughing with Shoshana. She shows him the red spots on her long feet. She pretends to be a nice ordinary person. She takes off her sandal and puts her long foot on a chair and shows him the spots and he nods. She has a hoarse voice that hides who she really is. Daddy is smart so how come she can fool him?

Between the Motion and the Act

Nat stood close to the kibbutz nurse in order to absorb the ebbing current that emanated from her body. After she was gone, he turned to Rubin, tanned and smiling under his Pioneer hat, and asked, "Why do we do it?"

"Do what?"

"Run after women."

"Biological urge, I think."

"If our wives did the same thing we wouldn't like it."

"That's true."

"You know what I think, Rubin? I think that if I knew Avra would always be loyal I'd make a commitment to be monogamous."

"You're joking! Judging by the six lookers I know about, you're no slouch."

"But …"

"No buts. I know you. Why did they give you fur-lined underpants on Purim? You know, Nat, I discovered that women are at their most vulnerable after the first child. Wait two months and you'll be able to get them all."[6]

Dori

Daddy leaves. It's not so bad though because either Daddy or Mummy will come back later to kiss me goodnight.

I'm the only one who's allowed a goodnight kiss. That's because in Canada we all slept in the same house and when we came back to Eldar I cried and screamed when Mummy tried to leave me in the Children's House. Even though the Minder[7] was Doreet. Doreet was my Minder before we left Eldar and for a short time when we came back.

Doreet was nice but I didn't want Mummy to leave. I held her shirt and wouldn't let go. Mummy said *she's having trouble getting used to the Children's House* and Doreet agreed.

Finally Mummy promised to come back later to kiss me goodnight. I stopped crying right away. I was so happy that she was coming back. So happy! Now I get a kiss every night.

The other children wish their parents could kiss them goodnight too. I don't really know why Mummy is allowed but somehow she got permission. I'm not complaining. It's not fair but I need it.

The Parent Clutch

Dori

Not too long ago I gave everyone in my Group[8] a colour.

Lulu is red. She has a red rash around her mouth and a very good heart. She shares the candies her parents give her on Friday with me—including the red ones that change the colour of your tongue. Actually I don't really like the red ones. They're too sharp.

Simon is green. He's chubby and he hardly ever says anything and also Daddy told me a story about a boy called Simon who wanted green hair.

Gilead is brown of course. He's tall and has brown skin. He doesn't have a father and he wasn't born on Eldar. There's a lot I don't know about Gilead.

Skye is very very dark blue. Her hair looks dark blue in the sun and the sky is dark blue at night and she's the most serious in our Group. Also the smartest.

Elan is white. His skin is white and his hair is almost white and he's skinny and scared. He's so scared he sometimes shakes like a ghost. I don't know if he has a mother but his father is a round jokey man who's crazy about my sister Sara. He calls her Suraleh.

Jonathan is yellow because he has yellow hair. He likes me.

Shoshana makes fun of the way Simon walks because he doesn't lift his feet. Every day she says *look how he walks! look how he walks!* and she wants everyone to laugh with her. But no one laughs. I don't know what's wrong with walking any way you want.

Our First Year

13 January 1949. Last night was our farewell party at Ein Hashofet. The Dining Hall was packed: long white tables loaded down with cakes, candies and later, coffee; a sea of familiar faces; speeches;

readings, including a satirical but friendly study of the idiosyncrasies of the gang; on all the walls beautiful photos of our life here; two original dances prepared by our modern dance group; folk-dancing and singing with a rip-roaring spirit until two a.m.; culminating in a wild hora that had the walls quivering. After that we finished loading trucks, by starlight, and left in a convoy for Eldar at five in the morning.

The ride was extremely cold, and when we reached the Galilee, the roads became tortuous and the wind cutting and icy. We rode through a landscape of majestic mountains, red earth in some sections practically turgid with fertility, and monstrous rocks, bulbaceous and knotty.

Eldar itself squats on a hill, white, silent, about 900 meters above sea-level, with its mosque and surrounding dwellings stuck right into the contours of the elevation, as if pushed tightly and economically into place by the finger of a giant. A Shell gasoline pump stands at the foot of the road leading to the village, a grotesquely modern totem in the midst of the red-grey mountains. To the north, quite a distance away in Lebanon, and as white and awesome as something out of Tibet or Alaska, looms the snow-covered Mount Hermon, a magnificent view.

By the time most of the vehicles had arrived, there were nearly 200 people present, and we immediately began laying the foundation for the Dining Hall. Prefab sections, tools, pots, sacks, trunks, beds, picks, shovels, and touriyas[9] and boards were moving and swinging in all directions. Reporters and cameramen seemed to be as thick as flies.

At noon the work was interrupted and the official ceremonies were conducted. Flags and coloured banners beat violently in the wind. There were cakes, oranges and wine. The army men who had been stationed there up to our arrival walked around with rifles slung casually from the shoulder over greatcoats and sheepskins. It could have been opening night at the Met, only in the opposite, non-bourgeois direction of course.

When the celebration was over, the guests began to leave, and the kibbutzniks got down to business, began to get settled for the night, took over military positions, cleaned out some of the deserted buildings on the edge of the village, and assigned work duties. "It's all yours," the soldiers said as they pulled out. "It's all yours."

Dori

Everyone is already sitting at the two round tables. I'm the last one. Lulu waves at me. I sit down next to her and she gives me a hug. She has curly hair that matches her name. Lulululululu sounds like a lot of curls. It goes back to where it started like a circle and curls are circles too.

For supper there's bread and margarine and green beans and beet soup and cheese triangles. No soup bits[10] unfortunately. We don't get soup bits that often. My three favourite foods in the world are figs from a tree—not the dried kind—and pomegranates and soup bits. You can't get any of those foods in Canada. It's too cold to grow figs and pomegranates there and they don't know how to make soup bits.

My favourite dessert is chocolate leben but today there's carrots and raisins.

The carrots and raisins are never the same. Sometimes the carrots are sweet and thin and there's just the right amount of water and the raisins are big and delicious and the water gets sweet from the raisins. Other times the carrots are in big pieces and they taste bitter and the raisins are small and yellow and sour and there's so much water you can't taste anything. I wish the Kitchen would get it right all the time.

Thane of Eldar

Here stands Jeremiah ben Jacob, sometime of London, risen to Thane, that eats the swimming frog, the toad, the tadpole, the wall-newt and the water. The rats however I am killing. Peace, Smulkin!

Dori

Shoshana doesn't notice that I'm not drinking my milk. That's one good thing about Shoshana—she never notices what anyone eats or drinks. She's too busy at the sink. I pour my milk into Gilead's cup. He likes everything.

I only like milk when there's cocoa in it. The cocoa in Canada is different from the cocoa in Eldar. In Canada it's sweeter and you can make it yourself. You have to squish the pieces that float up and you can add a little more if it isn't sweet enough though it's harder to squish when the milk is already in the cup. The cocoa in Canada is called Quik. Here they make the cocoa in the Kitchen. It's not as good as Quik but it's better than no cocoa.

Hot cocoa sometimes has skin that you have to take off with your spoon. I would die if I had to eat the skin. Or lumps in semolina. Or soft-boiled eggs. Semolina is very hard to make without lumps. Every time Shoshana brings semolina from the Kitchen I get worried. Sometimes you bite on a lump by mistake because you can't see it. I try not to eat semolina at all. It's not worth it.

Hard to believe but Simon likes the skin on hot milk. That's because his parents like it.

Shoshana says whoever is good can help her wash the dishes. She thinks we're dummies. Pioneers have to work hard but we're only children. Why would we want to help her wash dishes?

But Simon does. He stands on a chair and dries the dishes. He looks funny with an apron on because he's round. I whisper to Lulu *aprons look funny on round people* and we laugh until our stomachs hurt.[11]

Archaeology

House of the Second Mukhtar of the village of El-Daar (1872–1948); now an archaeological museum containing artefacts found in the vicinity.

"The Hyksos built a village here a little less than six thousand years ago; I ran into their village when I dug the foundation for the high school. We found one of their graves with some lovely Middle Bronze Age pottery. After the Hyksos came the Canaanites; they turned Eldar into a walled village. We found very good pottery with glazed decorations, and one of the altars on which they sacrificed children twice a year. The Israelites came next; they built a fort here. They were technologically primitive but monotheistic. The Assyrians wiped Eldar out in 722 BCE; we found a layer of ashes; it was burnt. The Babylonian and Persian conquests don't show up here at all. The Greeks show up, however; the army of Alexander the Great probably built an army outpost here. And then the Romans came—we have thousands of Roman coins. During the late Roman period Eldar was a Jewish village. We found a synagogue, a ritual bath, twelve burial caves. The cave opposite the chicken house was identified by the Talmudic rabbis as belonging to Rabbi Sisi. The Byzantine period was very strong here. We haven't found a church, but the Byzantines often used the synagogues as churches. Just yesterday we ran into a whole Byzantine complex and an Israelite complex below it. The bull-dozer cut a cross-section, you can see it all. After the Byzantines we have the early Arab period, 7th to 10th century. Then came the Crusades; Eldar was a small Crusader outpost with three large forts nearby. Then of course we have the Egyptian conquest; we found some beautiful Mameluke jewellery here from the 13th century. After that, the Turks ruled the region but the population remained Arab. During the British Mandate, Eldar was a head-quarters for the commander of the Palestine Liberation Army. That's why Eldar was raided in 1948. The villagers left overnight and Eldar became an army outpost on 29 October. We arrived two months later, on 13 January, to found the kibbutz. The belongings of the Arab villagers, what they had not taken with them that night, lay scattered all over the place."[12]

Dori

We're supposed to conserve water because water is scarce in our land. But Shoshana doesn't care. At first it looks as if she cares because she turns the water off for the soap part. We cover ourselves from top to bottom with the soap. Every time it slips out of our hands we laugh and yell *it slipped it slipped.*

When we're finished Shoshana turns the water back on. She's supposed to keep it on just enough to get the soap off but she lets us shower for as long as we want so I don't know why she turned it off for the soap part. We get a little wild. Shoshana doesn't care about that either. She's not in the room.[13]

Finally she shuts off the water and we get our towels from the hooks on the wall. There's a piece of sticking plaster over my hook with my name on it. I can't read it yet but I like seeing my name there. And I love sticking plaster. It smells good. Dafna the nurse lets me have the metal reels when they're finished because she knows how much I like them. How does she know? I can't remember. Maybe Daddy told her. She also gives me the tiny bottles with the rubber caps that you put needles into. I love those bottles.

In Canada they have Band-Aids that don't hurt when you take them off. Mummy bought me a book in a train station in Canada that had two real Band-Aids in the back. *Nurse Nancy*. There wasn't much of a story and the pictures weren't very good but I loved the Band-Aids. On my birthday in Canada my aunt asked me what I wanted and I said *Nurse Nancy* so I could get two more Band-Aids. Daddy didn't like that I got a book that was exactly the same as a book I already had but I was very happy. My old grandmother came to look after us while Daddy and Mummy went out and I put one of the Band-Aids on her finger where the top part was missing. I forget what I did with the other one.

Plaster hurts a lot when you take it off. Shoshana pulls it off very fast. Pulling it off fast hurts more—but at least it only hurts for a second. Does Shoshana do it the fast way because it hurts more or because it only hurts for a second? I don't know. I prefer the slow way.

In Canada children take baths instead of showers and after the bath you get a big soft towel. All you have to do

is pat the towel a little on your body. Pioneers rub themselves dry with a small thin towel. I like the Pioneer way
better. Pioneers are important. We're building our land.

Our First Year

16 January 1949. I'm so tired I can hardly keep my eyes open (it
seems as if we've been awake for the last three days straight). I've
just returned from the shower room where I met Naftali, who tells
me that tomorrow we receive military training for guard duty.
Syria and Trans-Jordan are in our backyard.

The wind is now blowing more powerfully, and it whispers
loudly, like a thousand lips shushing high up in the sky, as it sifts
through the Poinciana, eucalyptus, and pepper trees. The moon
shines down on a piece of wall, a burnt-out house, a pile of rubble,
a tile floor without walls and ceiling. In the weaving moonlight one
can almost see the ghosts of the spirited life that flourished here.

I am thinking of the deserted village of Eldar, which we entered
so proudly and energetically this morning, and the lives of the
Arabs who lived here. I wandered through some of the hovels,
looked at the overturned jugs, grain, books, baby shoes, and
smelled the smell of destruction. Are we also destroying, pillaging,
being cruel in this ancient land, with our ideals and our refusals
to stoop to the world's rottenness? Perhaps. We have moved into
Eldar; it is ours; we are responsible for our acts, even though we
are bound under the direction and discipline of our Movement.
But do we have an alternative? Can we step aside, refuse to be
morally sullied by Eldar and demand some other section of our
Homeland on which to build our homes? I do not think so.

We are not responsible for this cruel and forced contradic-
tion; we would prefer to disown it if we could; we bear no hatred
towards the Arab workers and peasants.

But we have been forced into a position where we must fight
for our lives and the lives of our people, and today life is largely
determined by frontiers, and frontiers must be defended no matter what the price. We do not have the right to shunt this moral

and political responsibility off on others. The kibbutz that we build at Eldar will be dedicated not only to the renaissance of our own people, but to mankind and the future of mankind. And this includes our Arab neighbours.

Dori

We have two bedrooms. I'm in the one with Skye and Elan and Simon.

My bed is next to the wall between the bedrooms. Right where Lulu's bed is on the other side.

Elan is in the corner after me and Simon is in the corner after Elan and Skye is in the corner near the door. When the door opens Shoshana can't see Skye right away. If Skye is sitting up in bed she has time to get under the blanket.

We take our pyjamas out of our drawer. In Canada people keep their pyjamas squished up under their pillow but Pioneers don't have pillows. We're supposed to fold our pyjamas but I don't know why. I understand about the pillows but not the folding. We don't need pillows. But pyjamas are just for sleeping in. Who cares if they're squished?

We get into bed and Shoshana says goodnight. This could be a bad part but it's not so bad for me because I'm waiting for my goodnight kiss. We're not supposed to talk. If we talk Shoshana might come back and get mad.

One of the rhymes I like is Who Keeps Barking All the Time—

> *Who keeps barking all the time?*
> *It's that little dog of mine.*
> *He guards us with all his might*
> *Good night, he says. Sleep tight.*

What I really love is the picture that goes with that rhyme. It's a picture of a Children's House in another kibbutz. The children there are luckier than us. They're allowed to get up and go to the window. Their Minder isn't Shoshana. And they have a dog. No wonder they're happy. I love the aqua in that picture. Aqua is my favourite colour.

Except for Friday we're not even allowed to talk after Shoshana leaves. If she comes back and finds us talking we'll be in trouble. Sometimes we take a chance but not tonight. Tonight no one has anything to say and it's quiet. There's a potty in the middle of the room in case someone has to pee. Elan sometimes pees in his sleep. He can't help it.

It's dark outside and very quiet. We can hear the jackals in the mountains. I love that sound. *Ah-woooooooo.* Jackals don't like humans but they're too far to reach us. Just like the Enemy. The Enemy is dangerous no matter what but most animals won't bother you if you don't bother them. Unless they're hungry and you're the only food.

The Other Children's House

Dori

I suck my finger while I wait for my kiss. My brother David sucks two fingers but I only suck one. Some children suck their thumb but with me it's always my first finger. That finger is already flatter than the first finger on my other hand. I know I'll stop when I'm older but I don't know when. David is ten and he still sucks his fingers.

I like to touch something soft while my finger is in my mouth. Under my eye for example—especially if I squish the skin a little with my thumb. Or I can flap my earlobe back and forth. They're both good. Eye or ear. The main thing is that my finger is in my mouth. I can't help sucking my finger. It's not up to me.

It's really quiet outside. Big and dark and quiet. When when when will Mummy or Daddy come?

The Good Fairy

Dori

Here she is! Here she is finally! Mummy comes to my bed. Everyone is jealous. She doesn't say anything to the other children. I wish she'd say goodnight to everyone but she doesn't. She sits on my bed and only talks to me. I know it's not fair but I can't help being happy. Very very happy.

Usually she has a song or a rhyme for me. She knows a lot of rhymes by heart because she's a teacher. She loves rhymes. Her favourite is Four Ostriches Said—

> *Four ostriches said*
> *Let us visit the pheasants*
> *How good it will be*
> *To bring lots of presents*
>
> *Four ostriches sighed*
> *Our visit was pleasant*
> *Too bad we forgot*
> *To bring all the presents*

Mummy laughs. I can't say I know exactly why this rhyme makes her laugh. I wouldn't be happy if I forgot to bring a present. But I'm happy that Mummy's laughing.

I know everyone else is listening too. They're jealous but they can't help liking the rhymes. Mummy says *one more and then I have to go.* She chooses a very plain rhyme. It's so plain I don't even know why it's in a book. Anyone can come up with a rhyme like that—

> *Winter's here*
> *Down comes the rain*
> *Look! Raindrops on*
> *The window pane*

Then she kisses me again and leaves. Now I'm alone like everyone else but at least Mummy came.

Thy Neck with Chains of Gold[14]

Characters:

> RITA, a teacher in her late twenties, currently working as Minder of the eight-year-olds, including Michael and Marina's son Efraim (Effie).

RICKY, a short, balding man in his late twenties who is courting Rita.

MICHAEL, a tall, brilliant high-school teacher in his mid-thirties, father of Lila, 3, and Efraim (Effie), 8.

MARINA, a high-strung woman in her mid-thirties, married to Michael.

ELI, the work coordinator.

Note: The characters were born in North America and speak English.

Time: The late fifties.

Place: A remote, northern kibbutz in Israel.

Scene: RITA's cabin room, containing a single bed, small table, chair, two shelves for a kettle, dishes, hotplate, etc., a black kerosene stove for heating, vase with wildflowers, photos and prints on the wall. MICHAEL and MARINA's room is next door but not seen. As the play opens, RITA is washing the floor of her room with a mop and pail. RICKY stands at the doorway watching her.

RICKY   It's a bit late for washing floors, isn't it?

RITA   I couldn't take a break today. The children in my Group are sick. My hotplate broke and I had to run to the kitchen for boiled water. There's been no laundry for three days because of the rain and I'm drying their clothes on the stove. I'm stuck in the Children's House with them all day and they're cranky. I thought they'd never fall asleep.

RICKY   *(takes mop from her)* Let me.

RITA   As you like.

RICKY   Of course I like. Anytime you need a mopping job done, just call on Ricky.

RITA   *(shaking a mat outside)* This mud—where does it all come from?

RICKY   Tomorrow it won't rain.

RITA   How do you know?

RICKY	Oh, I have many fine qualities. I'm a good floor-washer, I can predict the weather, I'm kind, generous and considerate, and I do fifty-four push-ups a day. *(Does push-ups)* 16, 27, 62, 54 … Can you think of anything else?
RITA	No. *(She steps over him to replace mat)*
RICKY	I'm a good nudnik.
RITA	You can say that again. *(She makes up her bed)*
RICKY	I'm a good nudnik. (RITA *groans.* RICKY *mops about her feet, trying to attract her attention)* Halva, the crazy red cow, finally calved. Guess what she had? Triplets! … Well—a calf, anyway … And I found a Roman coin in the valley. *(Shows her)* Gila burnt the soup today and threw the whole pot at Yossi. She blamed him for not watching it.
RITA	So what else is new?
RICKY	Eli wants to do away with Nebuchadnezzar. The poor donkey broke a leg. Do you think it's humane? *(rifle shots audible)*
RICKY	*(holds up stick)* Boom boom … The army is here.
RITA	On a night like this, it's not much fun to be on guard.
RICKY	Unless you're on guard with me.

Dori

More *Pinocchio*. I love the pictures in this book.[15] The puppet-master is huge and has two green snakes twisted around his whip and his eyes are red. I like the picture of Geppetto in the snow and Pinocchio eating the apple peels. I love the picture where the fairy is carrying two jugs. The Arab women have those kind of jugs. Sometimes they balance them on their heads. I wouldn't be able to do that no matter how much I practised. But I wouldn't mind having a jug.

I only like some parts of *Pinocchio*. I like the puppet show and the funfair and the donkey ears. I like when his nose grows and the whale and the buried treasure. I feel bad for him that he got tricked. It wasn't his fault.

What I don't like is when Pinocchio buries his head in the ground. I told Daddy to skip that part.

My brother David comes in and Daddy says he has to go out for a few minutes. David thinks of something to do. He decides to put some of Mummy's skin lotion on his peenie. He wants it to have a good smell.

David Playing with String

Dori

Mummy comes into the Room with my sister Sara. Sara is screaming and crying. She wants something but no one knows what it is. She repeats a word over and over but we can't understand what she's saying. We offer her everything we can think of but she goes on crying and screaming and saying the word.

One time Mummy was carrying Sara down the long hallway of our house on Davaar Street and I pinched Sara's foot and she cried. It was my first time being mean. My first and so far my last time. Mummy turned around and said *Dori are you doing anything to Sara?* and I said *no* but as soon as Mummy turned her head I pinched Sara's foot again and she cried again.

Now I feel bad about what I did. Sometimes I see Sara in the yard of the Toddlers' House and her face is the saddest face I've ever seen. I want to bite her sad cheeks but it would hurt her. I want to bite them and eat them but all I can do is look. It's not enough.

Our First Year

17 January 1949. Our immediate and most aggravating specific problem is Hebrew. Without Hebrew you're lame, blind, and frustrated; and we have many comrades, especially newcomers, who can hardly say 'yes' and 'no' in the holy tongue.

Another routine problem is that of inexperience in kibbutz administration. The completely free and democratic set-up leads to many subtle problems of efficiency and procedure, which often assume delicate human angles.

The weekly Meeting,[16] for instance—and it deserves the capital letter—is the most sacred, the most complex, and the most easily violated of the institutions of kibbutz. It is the chief organ of democratic procedure in which every member of the kibbutz stands as an equal and has the right to express his or her views on any and every subject. All committees, institutions, and individuals must bow before the decisions of the Meeting. The Meeting is the dynamic and intangible repository of the philosophy of kibbutz collectivism.

Quite obviously such an institution cannot be mastered within a few days. In my opinion some of our Meetings are miserable failures. There are endless repetitions of the same point; lengthy, vapid speeches; undisciplined and prejudiced expressions of opinions; a senseless burrowing into detail. The Meeting is a sort of extremely complex and monumental fugue in which a large number of the motifs of kibbutz life are brought together in what must be an aesthetic and productive composition, and if some of these motifs get out of hand, they produce a clattering and painful discord in the close counterpoint. This evening we discussed everything from whether or not babies should be picked up when they cry to the price of onions in California.

Often somebody has to sound out an individual or a problem beforehand, in order to prevent an uncomfortable and aggravating impasse during the Meeting. Certain simple procedural rules must be strictly followed, otherwise the democratic nature of the discussion may be intolerably violated.

Our third problem is recruitment. We have composed an appeal that will appear in the next issue of the YG periodical Youth and Nation:

> We, the Pioneers of Eldar, demand as Jews that the entire façade of the cracked and crumbling mausoleum that is bourgeois society be ripped down and replaced with a new socialist structure based on spiritual and economic egalitarianism. Here we will create the new man and the new child, for whom collectivist values and high moral standards are natural and innate. We appeal to those who cannot warm themselves under the bright glow of an illusion. Join with us, struggle, and build.

Dori

Daddy holds my hand and we walk towards the Children's House. Luckily he meets some people and stops to talk to them. If I'm very lucky it will be a long conversation.

I don't know too many people on Eldar. I only know my Group and Daddy and Mummy and my sister Sara and my brother David and his two friends Noam and Amnoni and Amnoni's sister Hagar because they're twins and Coco because she has a shaggy dog and Dafna the nurse and Lulu's father and mother and Mummy's friend Edna who was my Minder when I was a baby. I also know Doreet who was my Minder before Shoshana but for some reason I never see Doreet. And I know Elan's father. He's the round jokey man who loves Sara.

Wait—there's also Simon's mother Nina. She does afternoon Wake-Up a lot of the time. She's very nice. She works in the laundry.

The only other adult I know is Shoshana. Unfortunately.

Baby Diary

Born: 30 Sivan, 5715/June 20, 12:00
Weight: 3.450
Length: 52 cm.
Came home on 23 June.

June 20–29
I have a sweet, pretty daughter. She looks a little like my family, a little like David. Every day she grows and develops. She has blue

eyes, blonde hair, a round face, a button nose, a sweet mouth. Her body is long. She lifts her head when lying on her stomach. She has the strength to kick and throw off her diaper when she demands food.

On the third day after she came back, the bellybutton fell. It's still a bit moist and protruding. It's been covered with Dermetol and a cloth belt.

She feeds seven times a day. For the first few days she fed every three hours. Yesterday and today she began to feed every three and a half to four hours. At night she gets a bottle half-filled with milk for her seventh feeding.

At first when she woke up between feedings she was given water. Water in general calms her. I feel now after nine days that I have more milk and she really does wait longer between feedings. She latches on firmly and well. She's already found her thumb and has sucked it three times!

Edna L. is her Minder. She's very good and dedicated. At the beginning, when I was very weak, she really helped me.

Naftali is on Guard Duty. He gives her the last bottle. There's a good chance she'll give up that bottle early.

Dori

We sing a song going back—

> *The voice of dodi*
> *The voice of dodi*
> *The voice of dodi behold it comes*
> *Leaping over the mountains*
> *Skipping upon the hills*

I'm not sure what *dodi* means. I don't think anyone would write a poem about the voice of their uncle. But the words are from long ago and Hebrew was a little different then. Daddy calls me *doda* even though I'm his daughter not his aunt so I know it's something else too.

The two other names I get called are sweetie and dolly. I asked Daddy why he calls me *doda* but he didn't know how to explain it.[17]

The first part of the song isn't very serious and you can sing it with a hiccup. *The voice of dodi*—hic! *The voice of dodi*—hic! My brother David taught me that. But the second part suddenly gets sad and beautiful and full of longing.

Longing is something I feel quite a lot of. Especially when I look past the mountains. I long for something that's going to happen some day in the future. Something wonderful and exciting that I can't even imagine now. Like Ali Baba saying *abracadabra, sea and sand, take us to another land* and then finding caskets overflowing with jewels. Something magic but real.

A Good Tan

— Why did you stay on Eldar?
— I've always wanted to have a good tan. Working outdoors all day guarantees an excellent tan.
— Is that the real reason?
— Yes.[18]

Dori

Daddy finishes talking to the person he met. I'm very hungry today. I think it's because we had bellybuttons[19] for lunch. There isn't much food on a bellybutton. It's the same with chicken throats and feet but they're mostly for sucking or putting in soup. Bellybuttons we get on a plate. There was scrambled egg too but it was too soft. And mashed something that no one ate.

Daddy comes into the Children's House with me. I see that there's bread with margarine already on the table but Shoshana says to wait until the food's ready. Daddy's there though—so she can't do anything. On top of that she's busy talking to him. I take a big bite out of the bread and then another until I finish the whole piece. I love bread and margarine.

Supper tonight is sardines and lettuce and very good potatoes and boring kidney beans. Lulu doesn't like the beans either. I spill a drop of milk on Lulu's beans. Just as a joke. Lulu laughs and spills some of her juice on my beans. Jonathan spills a bit of milk into my juice cup. Everyone starts to spill things.

Shoshana sees what's going on and gets angry. She yells at us *that's it a two minute shower and bed! look at this mess! what kind of children are you?*

She grabs Lulu's arm and pulls her to the shower. The rest of us follow fast so we won't get pulled too. Lulu's crying *ow ow ow*. Shoshana turns on the water for our shower and pulls off Lulu's clothes. We take off our own clothes as fast as we can. We go into the shower but before we even have a chance to put on soap Shoshana says *that's it* and turns the water off. She tells us we have two minutes to brush our teeth and put on pyjamas and line up for the toilet. We do everything she says.

Shoshana isn't allowed to pull Lulu. And she isn't allowed to hit us. That's a rule on Eldar. No hitting children. No hitting anyone.

Shoshana doesn't follow that rule.

Thy Neck with Chains of Gold

RICKY   Are you visiting your cousin in Haifa this week?
RITA   Why do you want to know?
RICKY   Is Michael giving you a lift?
RITA   Only to the bus stop. If I go.
RICKY   You could invite your cousin to come here sometimes.

RITA	What for?
RICKY	So I could meet him. I mean, any relative of yours might be a relative of mine. Give me a rag. *(To stuff along window sill)*
RITA	*(hands him a rag)* He works. His wife has small children. Why don't you leave me alone?
RICKY	You're very devoted to them—giving up your one day of rest.
RITA	Yes, I am.
RICKY	*(looks at window)* Now your room can brave the foulest storm. All you need is Ricky the Ragman. *(RITA turns to leave the room. RICKY blocks her way.)*
RITA	Will you let me go out?
RICKY	What for?
RITA	I have to pee, if you don't mind.
RICKY	Sure, why didn't you say so? *(Opens door for her)* *(RITA puts on her boots. MARINA appears in the doorway)*
MARINA	Rita, I want to talk to you.
RITA	Do you mind if I go to the outhouse first? *(Exits)* *(MARINA enters the room. Sees RICKY who checks the stove)*
MARINA	What's wrong with her?
RICKY	It has something to do with the relative positions of the sun and moon. *(MARINA sits)* Sit down, Marina, make yourself at home. I hear Effie's sick.
MARINA	Yes. I couldn't bring him to the Room. Lila cried because I kept running to the Children's House. There's only one of me and a family is entitled to two parents. I'll get Michael to quit driving that truck if it's the last thing I do!
RICKY	You can always call on an off-duty bachelor for assistance.
MARINA	Why doesn't some lucky girl marry you?
RICKY	How would you like to be my matchmaker? I'm interested in a dark-eyed beauty … *(draws a shape in the air)*
MARINA	I'll bet you even washed her floor. You know how Michael helps me, uh? By making a mess. He walks

31

into the room with his boots on; never uses an ashtray; and the day he'll put his clothes away you'll know the Messiah has arrived.

(RITA *enters. She plugs in kettle and warms her hands over stove*)

MARINA   It's true I'm only Effie's mother, and I've no right to bother you with stupid questions after working hours but I've got to know what the nurse said.

RITA   It's a cold.

MARINA   Maybe it's jaundice.

RITA   She said it's a cold.

MARINA   Are you giving him medicine?

RITA   Yes.

MARINA   Is he taking it?

RITA   Yes.

MARINA   I just looked in on him. He can hardly breathe.

RITA   *(hoping she won't have to go out)* He's not up, is he?

MARINA   No.

RITA   *(relieved)* I sang every song in the book until those kids fell asleep.

MARINA   You should sleep in the Children's House.

RITA   I told the Guard to check every half hour.

MARINA   Supposing he wakes between visits and cries?

RITA   It isn't the first time a child has had a cold in this kibbutz.

MARINA   If you were a mother, you wouldn't be so unfeeling.

RITA   Who wants a candy?

Dori

Very quiet. Shoshana's gone.

I whisper *Skye?* She whispers back *yes.* I whisper *Shoshana was angry.* She whispers *yes.* I whisper *do you think the Enemy is too far to reach us or we're too strong for them to reach us?*

She says *they're not far—you can walk to the border.* I ask *so they won't reach us because we're strong?* Skye says *we have Border Guards with rifles and if the Enemy manages to sneak past the Border Guards we have Guards here.*

That reminds me of something from long ago. It's the only thing I remember from before we left Eldar. I threw up on my bed in the middle of the night. I began to cry and the Night Guard[20] came in. He wanted to help but he didn't know where the clean sheets were. Just that day I noticed Doreet putting sheets in a laundry bag hanging from a nail. I thought how lucky that was because I noticed the bag for the first time that day. But when I showed the Guard the bag it was empty. He was nice but he didn't know much about children. Finally he told me to sleep near the edge of the bed. It wasn't a very good solution but there was nothing else to do so that's what I did.

Baby Diary

June 29
Dori has given up her seventh feeding. Today I gave her five feedings and Naftali gave her a bottle at night. She now eats every four hours—7, 11, 3, 7, 11.

Dori

Simon's mother is doing the afternoon Wake-Up. She never says much. She's the opposite of Shoshana.

Simon calls his mother Nina. It's funny. If I called my parents Naftali and Varda how would anyone know I was their daughter? Even we wouldn't know.[21]

Nina gives us a bag of treats because it's Friday. The treats are always a bit disappointing. The candies are plain and the piece of chocolate is hard. And the cookies are the boring kind you give little babies. The only thing I like is the cream wafers but there aren't any today.

I take my bag of treats and run as fast as I can to the Room. Daddy's happy to see me. I sit next to him on the sofa and we read *Pinocchio*.

The only picture I don't like in *Pinocchio* is the one at the end when Pinocchio becomes a boy. That boy looks very strange. He's too skinny and I don't like his clothes or anything else.

But I'm glad that Pinocchio's going to turn into a real boy. I'm tired of waiting for his troubles to be over. It's just one thing after another with Pinocchio. So when it's time to go back I ask Daddy to read the last page. I want him to read the rest of the story next time but right now I want to hear the last page.

Daddy says *I'll read you a whole other chapter instead.* He really doesn't like reading the end before you get there. But I don't give in so he reads the end and then he says *we have to go.*

Now I'm sorry I didn't give in because I could have had a whole other chapter which would have taken much longer.

I'm so sorry I feel sick.

Our First Year

18 January 1949. Woke up at 5:30 today, crawled over our beds, and stumbled down the road to the kitchen to put in a day's work. The weather is absolutely miserable. There's a pool of water in the middle of our room, and surrounding this pool are the beds of twelve people.

At present I'm hunched over a fireplace which produces more smoke than heat, and there are five people packed on either side of me so that I haven't the elbow room to wield a pencil in my icy fingers. My knees are warm but the rest of me is cold.

But wot-the-hell, it's been a wonderful day! We're started, on our own land, and the exhilaration can't be stamped out by all the hail and sleet in Greenland. Martin, sitting next to me, is trying to read a pamphlet on sub-tropical fruits. That's Eldar optimism.

We've set up three guard posts: at our entrance, at the north-east, and at the north-west of the village ... too exhausted and cold to continue writing.

Dori

Soup bits tonight! Only one spoon each though. I don't know why we can't have more. Also a slice of cake because it's Friday. Half chocolate half plain. It's a bit dry but so what.

In the shower Skye says to Shoshana *you promised we could wash our own hair this week.* And then everyone says *yes you promised you promised* even though I can't really remember any promise.

Shoshana has no choice. She has to let us. I don't know why Skye wants to wash her own hair but I want to because Skye wants to.

I've been hearing lately that if you keep your head up and back instead of down the soap on your hair won't get in your eyes. You think the soap will get in less if your face is down but it seems it's better to keep it up.

You have to be a little brave to lift your face because what if it doesn't work? I gather my courage and do it. I think it works.

Transcript of Meeting
April 1961

Topic: Status of Jeremiah Ben-Jacob
Chair: Isaac Milman

Isaac: First on the agenda: Coco and Varda claim, among other things, that "Jeremiah Ben-Jacob is a danger to health, does not contribute sufficiently to the kibbutz, is not a member, has not requested to be considered for membership, and should be asked to leave Eldar." Specific reference was made to Jeremiah's attempt to enter the Kitchen after lying on a pile of manure.

Naftali: I saw him carrying a rat by its tail—who knows where he was going.

Martin: He likes garbage. He does a good job collecting all the garbage—a job no one else especially wants.

Coco: That's hardly enough work to justify his expenses.

Martin: What expenses? He sleeps in the ruins on a pile of hay, never asks for new clothes, and eats whatever you give him. He never complains, unlike some people I could mention.

Nina: I do feel that he should not be given the job of delivering clean laundry on the donkey.

Isaac: If I may go one step further, I also don't think he should be allowed to eat in the Dining Hall. No one wants to sit next to him or handle anything he's touched, and with good reason.

Varda: I agree—it's extremely unsanitary. We have enough health issues as it is. I'd like to hear Dafna's professional opinion about the health hazard he poses to the community.

Dafna: I don't know that he has anywhere to go. I don't think he has anyone in England … he said something to that effect, though I didn't entirely understand … We should remember that he was a well-known Shakespearean actor once.

Varda: Once was once. I was Queen Esther once. Now he's dotty.

Martin: I find it offensive to think that our community can't find a place for the infirm. If we can't do that, then we are all hypocrites and elitists and this entire enterprise is a farce.

Lou: I agree completely. What happened to social justice, brotherhood and freedom?

Edna:	I feel that if someone talks to him and explains that he can't enter the Kitchen or Dining Hall unless he's spic and span, he'll stay away.
Varda:	That flea-bitten coat of his makes me nervous.
Isaac:	Last time I came across him, he told me he was Thane of Eldar.
Martin:	"So foul and fair a day I have not seen."
Isaac:	Where's that from, *Hamlet*?
All:	*Macbeth!*
Naftali:	The reality is that we operate on a principle of membership and contribution. If he were a member, of course we'd make every allowance and try to help him. But he was sent here as a work volunteer and he's not working. How can we survive if we take on every vagrant who wanders in, regardless of what they contribute? We're not a hobo camp.
Ora:	I agree with Naftali. It's down to economics. We're struggling to feed ourselves—we simply can't afford to be a charity for the mentally ill at this point. As it is we're supporting forty-two city children whose costs are only half covered. A line has to be drawn somewhere.
Martin:	The children again! Every time we need an excuse not to do something, it's back to the children. I've said it a million times and I'll say it again: we are not doing these children a favour, they are doing *us* a favour by allowing us to raise them, which is a privilege and as far as I understand, the whole point of our existence.
Isaac:	I feel we're getting off topic here. We have to come to some decision about Jeremiah. Is that his real name, by the way?

Dori

We're finished drying ourselves with our towels. Gilead comes over and says *do you know how to make children?*

Of course I know. We're free on Eldar. It's different in Canada. People aren't free there. It's different in the city too. Also on airplanes and boats.

I say I know of course I know. He says do you want to do it?

I say *yes*. He touches my jinnie with his peenie. Shoshana is smiling. I'm surprised. I don't see her smiling too often—apart from when she talks to Daddy.

Sex in the Clubhouse

20 May 2002. Seven kibbutz boys aged nine to fourteen were discovered engaged in sodomy and other sexual acts by a concerned adult who forced the door to their clubhouse open after receiving no reply to his knocks. It appears the boys had been meeting regularly in the clubhouse for sex, usually in pairs but sometimes in groups. While kibbutzim generally prefer to handle legal matters internally, police became involved in the case when they were notified by the parents of the nine-year-old. The police are finding it difficult to lay charges as the acts seemed to have been consensual and the boys show no signs of distress.

Online comments:

> Don't believe this article, it's all a lie. There were developments today and more victims have been identified.

> That's what comes of kibbutz upbringing. They can change its name to Sodom and Gomorrah.

> Look in the prisons and tell me if you find a single kibbutz-born criminal.

> I know that boy well and he would never do anything like that, he isn't capable of it.

> Don't you have a life? It's a great kibbutz, I have many friends there, find something else to do.

I'm in the same grade as the 14-year-old and I want to say that most of us are behind him and forgive him for his mistake in spite of all the sadness and violence. And we hope he comes back to school as soon as possible. And I ask those who know nothing about it to stop commenting.

Stop believing this article, it was non-consensual, and there weren't seven boys, whoever believes this article is an idiot.

What is this country coming to?

We the kids of 8B support you and want you back.

Maybe now you see why I left the kibbutz and returned to God.

In my yeshiva I'm only allowed to get off with other yeshiva students.

With all the television children watch is it any wonder?

I left the kibbutz years ago and the stigma of licentiousness still follows me. It's completely unjustified.

This is all because not enough money goes to education, it's all going to the settlements and the religious.

Today's youth know how to enjoy themselves ...

I don't understand these jocular responses. Even if the relations were consensual it's appalling. It's nothing to do with these being homosexual acts. Sexual relations are not for children. This shows one thing only—serious emotional deficiency and specifically lack of parental warmth and attention starting in infancy. And to all those who are cracking jokes: there's a time and a place.

Ah the kibbutz, the kibbutz! Now everyone's shocked. They should just think back to what they did as kids to pass the time.

The law prohibits this for the simple reason that sexual acts cannot be consensual for minors and this includes adults who seduce boys who supposedly say 'yes'. The result is severe emotional damage for the rest of their lives.

The damage occurs when they grow up and face the intolerance of a society that dictates what is right and what should be.

Have all the pedophiles suddenly crawled out from under a rock??

Nu, really! This is nothing new. I grew up on a kibbutz many years ago, these types of events were common. With us the afternoon shower was a laboratory for experimentation; only in our case the police weren't involved and we had a blast and that's the way it should be.

Dori

Shoshana says she has a surprise for us. She says because we've been so good we're going to go on a Night Hike. We all begin to shout *Night Hike Night Hike!* We're very happy. We rush to put on our pyjamas and slippers.

Finally Shoshana says we can go. It's hot and dark outside. We walk two by two except for Simon and Elan and Skye who walk single file.

The bushes on both sides of the path have a wonderful sweet smell. You can see all the stars up in the sky and the Big Dipper and the Little Dipper. Actually I'm not sure I know which stars are the Little Dipper but I can definitely see the Big Dipper. The handle points to the North Star.

In case I ever get lost and I don't have a compass I can find my way by following the North Star.

We start singing—

> *Me and he and you*
> *And Yankele Kangaroo*
> *We went out for a walk*
> *So we could have a talk*
>
> *We walked hallah hallah*
> *Until we met Abdallah*
> *We punched him in the eye*[22]
> *And he began to cry*

There's another ending—

> *We walked hallah hallah*
> *Until we met Abdallah*
> *We said shalom*
> *And he began to cry*

But that ending doesn't rhyme. Some of us sing the ending with the punch and some of us sing the ending with shalom.

I know *yallah* is Arabic and I can also say it with an Arabic accent. Is *hallah* Hebrew for *yallah*? If we have a Hebrew word how come we mostly say *yallah*? Maybe *yallah* is more for telling someone to move. It's fun to say *yallah*. Especially with the accent. *Y'allah y'allah!* Let's get going. *Y'allah*.[23]

Baby Diary

July 1
She gave up her night bottle. I fed her at 11:30 and also at 4:00, so I'm giving her six feedings. From 6 to 9 P.M. she's restless. After that feeding she moans, cries, wants to be held. She's given water

and eventually falls asleep. Maybe she doesn't get enough food at this time or maybe her stomach hurts. During the day and after every other nursing she falls asleep easily, and sleeps very well between feedings.

Dori

Finally we reach the Dining Hall where the adults are having supper. We run to our parents. Daddy and Mummy are very happy to see me. They give me another piece of cake.

Then everyone sings In the Plains of the Negev. I don't know all the words but it's about a soldier who falls in the desert. His mother is crying but a tall lad comes over. He calls her Mother and tells her not to cry because her son was brave and fought the Enemy. And without brave soldiers like her son, the Enemy would break us. The song ends—

> *If you will it friends*
> *It is no dream*

It's a sad song with a sad tune. Even if another lad wants to be her son she's still going to miss the son who died. And even if her son died for our land he's still dead.

Herzl is the man who said *if you will it friends it is no dream*. Daddy likes to say those words.

One day I'll have to go to the army too. In other countries women don't go to the army but here we're equal. I'll try to be brave but I don't know if I'll succeed. Sometimes I'm brave and sometimes I'm not. When we went to the infirmary to get shots, Dafna the nurse asked *who wants to go first?* We all said we weren't afraid but no one wanted to go first. Finally I said *I'll be first* and I lay down on the table. Everyone was watching me and feeling scared but I didn't make a sound. I said *it doesn't hurt at all* and after that no one was scared. But that was only partly because I was brave and partly because I like Dafna. I felt that shot the whole rest of the day.

Actually we're not completely equal in the army. Women don't go to the front line. The truth is that I'm glad I won't have to go to the front line. If the Enemy starts shooting I'll be in the back row. It's not fair for the men to get killed instead of me but I can't help being glad. It's wrong but that's the way I feel. I don't want to die. Even for our land.

Thy Neck with Chains of Gold

MICHAEL *enters from porch. A knapsack hangs over his shoulders. His dress is picturesquely careless. Whistling, he knocks on* RITA's *door and opens it. Goes straight to* RITA, *then slowly turns around, sees his wife, laughs self-consciously and moves towards her.*

MICHAEL   Ah, here you are, sweetheart.

MARINA   You were looking for me, Michael?

MICHAEL   Yeah, you weren't in the room, so I figured you're here.

MARINA   *(nods skeptically)* Sure …

MICHAEL   Yeah, sure. *(kisses her cheek, puts the knapsack on the table, slaps* RICKY's *back in comradely fashion. During his speech he puts his rifle on* RICKY's *book.)* Did I have a day. You wouldn't believe it.

MARINA   No, I wouldn't.

MICHAEL   On the way to town, just as I'm taking one of those beautiful curves, I see something black on the road. I jam on the brakes and nearly fly off into the valley. And right there in front of me—a flock of goats—and the poor Arab kid is having a hell of a time getting them off the road. To make a long story short, when Eli finds out how many eggs were smashed, he'll have a fit. Anyhow,

I'm almost in Tel Aviv and wham—a flat. But no tragedy. Kibbutz Atar came to the rescue. They check my spare but it's no damn good so they give me a tire. I ask how much we owe them and the secretary says they don't expect our kibbutz to pay for anything. We still owe them twenty-one work-days from the time they helped us install our electricity. So—I get to Tel Aviv with broken eggs and I bump into Ramona. *(to* RICKY*)* She's as cute as ever—and she says she's lonesome for the kibbutz.

MARINA   I bet.

MICHAEL   So I tell her to come back and she says she visited once *(to* MARINA*)* and got the cold shoulder. So I bought her a sundae to cheer her up ... on the way back I drop in to see my friend the Mukhtar. We have some roast lamb and a drink. It's very important to keep on cordial relations with our Arab neighbours—so I had another drink. But just as I was leaving, the lousy truck stalls. I check the tires and I find the one Atar gave me is no good. The bastards! Just because we owe them twenty-one work days. So a tow truck takes me to the garage. They fix me up, and that's why I was late. And how was your day, Marina?

Dori

Daddy has to work in the Kitchen all day today so I can't see him until bedtime. Mummy is in the Room but she's busy with my sister Sara. I lie on the floor and look at the black book of paintings. I love that book. I simply love it.

My favourite painting is the one of the woman falling out of the tiger's mouth. There are bones and snakes spilling out too. I asked Daddy what the painting was about and he said it was a dream but I could tell he only said that because he didn't know how to explain it. I don't think he likes that painting very much.[24]

I look at it for a long time. Then I find the beautiful painting with the gas station. I like it as much as the tiger one. I want to be right inside that painting.[25]

After that I go in order. Some pictures are boring and I skip them. Others are very interesting. I try to figure out their story.

I ask Daddy which painting he likes best. He says he likes them all but I keep asking so he looks at the pictures and chooses the one that has two soldiers helping a woman nurse her baby. One soldier holds his canteen to her mouth and the other soldier helps her hold up the baby. She was probably dying but the soldiers saved her.[26]

I like canteens. My brother David has one. The water inside it tastes like metal. When I'm a soldier I'll carry a canteen wherever I go.

Our First Year

19 January 1949. The mosque was blown up today. Cloudy, drab day with bitter wind but no rain. A small group of us stood off to one side, way out of danger, with a beautiful view of the western wadi behind us, and this looming, softly curved and mysterious monument of a culture which none of us even begins to understand rising before us, its fate doomed within a matter of seconds.

There was a shattering explosion which shot a bolt of shock through each of us, wrenching our bodies with tension, and then the dome seemed to rise slowly into the grey sky, like a giant eggshell, with the steel reinforcing rods mangled and twisting out from the sides; it fell in pieces into the mass of earth and rubble and flying stone which was once the prince of Eldar's skyline.

Dori

Mummy takes my sister Sara to the Children's House. Then she comes back and we sing songs from a book I like. It's called *Uga Uga*. I know all the songs except for the train song which doesn't have a tune.

The pictures in the book are pretty but there's one I don't understand. It's for I've Been to Yemen—

> *I've been to Yemen*
> *And very soon*
> *The little black boy I met there*
> *Will be Ruthie's groom*

In the picture a little black boy in red and white shorts and a Yemenite hat is handing flowers to a much bigger girl in a wedding dress. It's only pretend so why is the boy dressed like someone from Yemen and why is he so little and why is Ruthie wearing a wedding dress and why is there a mosque like in Yemen and why is he black? I asked Mummy but she didn't understand the problem.[27]

We sing all the songs in the book and then Mummy takes me back to the Children's House. I don't beg for more time because with Mummy when it's time it's time and if you beg for more songs she only says *next time*.

At least she doesn't laugh with Shoshana the way Daddy does.

Baby Diary

July 7
She gets a bottle at night every second night. Today she followed Naftali's finger. And the next day [sic] she looked at a toy. I now have to rock her bed after almost every feeding. She moans, kvetches, lifts her head—after light rocking she falls asleep.

Between the third and fourth feeding she wakes up and cries and gets water and she falls asleep again. That happens every day at 5:00. Her bellybutton is already dry and perfectly fine.

During the day, at almost every feeding, Naftali comes to visit. She still eats every four hours and sleeps well during the day and is gaining nicely.

Dori

Shoshana is in a very bad mood today. For supper we have leben and cold beet soup and rice with carrots and cheese triangles. I can't decide if I like the cheese triangles or not. I like unwrapping them but I don't know if I like eating them.

We decide to have a contest to see who can have the pinkest pee. The more beet soup you drink, the pinker your pee is. We're going to check everyone's pee tonight to see who wins.

Dessert is apple sauce with cinnamon but everyone's too full from all the beet soup.

Shoshana gets angry that no one's eating their apple sauce. We can tell there's trouble coming but we don't know what it is.

Letter to the Editor
29 March 1961

I read with interest the article by K. Shabtai on Jews in Canada, including what Pomerantz, Editor of the Toronto Yiddish paper *The Forward,* had to say. As Pomerantz based his harsh words on the book by Naftali Satie, *Between the Motion and the Act* (or, according to him, *Between the Movement and the Act*), which he criticized and did not correctly evaluate in my opinion, I feel it incumbent upon me to right the wrong.

He wronged the author, first and foremost. Naftali Satie is one of the founders of Eldar, which borders on Lebanon. A year ago he finished writing *Between the Motion and the Act* and approached Vantage Press, which published it, not in paperback but in attractive hardback format. As soon as the book appeared it aroused great interest in Canada's literary and artistic community.

Pomerantz, and following him Shabtai, were shocked for some reason by the scene of coupling in the Christian cemetery in Montreal. Because Shabtai didn't read the book, my comments are directed mainly at Pomerantz. Firstly, the girl he refers to as a Christian prostitute is actually the young man's Jewish girlfriend. Secondly, they do not desecrate the grave of a youth killed in the war, but in fact weep over it. Finally, they do not have sex on the grave, or even near it.

If Pomerantz had read the book more objectively, and with a little less fear of "what the goyim will say," maybe he would have grasped its symbolic meaning. If an author attempts to expose, reveal and demonstrate, he must do so without arrogance, and if the Communists who left the Zionist movement are depicted as undergoing a spiritual crisis brought on by a lack of direction, then that is the way things are and nothing will come of silence.

—Zeev Tchornitski, *Davar*

Dori

The trouble comes. It mostly comes for Lulu.

We're all brushing our teeth at the sinks. Shoshana notices that Lulu isn't there. She's already in the bedroom putting on her pyjamas. Shoshana says *Lulu did you brush your teeth?* Lulu says *yes.* Shoshana checks Lulu's toothbrush and it's dry.

She grabs Lulu's arm and pulls her back to the room with the sinks and yells at her *is this toothbrush wet? is it wet? feel it feel it! is it wet?* Shoshana makes us feel the toothbrush. We're standing next to the wall and she asks us one by one to feel it and tell her if it's wet. We don't want to say but we have no choice. Shoshana yells at Lulu *you lied to me you lied to me!* She slaps Lulu twice on her face. Then she pulls her hair and throws her on the floor and begins to kick her with her sandal. Lulu screams. Shoshana kicks and yells *you lied.* If anyone on Eldar saw this they'd throw Shoshana out. But no one sees. No one but us.

Skye doesn't see either. She escaped to the bedroom when the trouble started.

No one says anything after Shoshana leaves. I suck my finger. Only instead of my eye or my ear the soft thing I touch tonight is my jinnie.

I wait and wait for my goodnight kiss. Finally Daddy comes. I'm so happy to see him! I sit up in bed and reach out my arms to him. He hugs me and kisses me and says he's sorry he missed me when I visited. He says *goodnight doda sweet dreams.* I tell him Shoshana hit Lulu but he only smiles and doesn't say anything.

Daddy doesn't really believe me. He has to believe me because he thinks you have to respect children but I can tell that even though he respects me and wants to believe me he doesn't believe me.

The truth is that Mummy once hit me too. It was in the house on Davaar Street.

I loved the house on Davaar Street. There was a long long hall with the kitchen at the end and there was a living room with a big window and a television and a record player and a couch. Mummy and Daddy slept in a bedroom that was right next to the bedroom I shared with my brother David. Their bed was between two doors. I don't know why that bedroom had two doors. They both led to the same place.

At first I could do whatever I wanted in Canada. But then Mummy took me to a building and inside there was a room and inside the room there were a lot of crowded children. A very old woman came over and said *shalom Dori*. That was all the Hebrew she knew. The rest was in English.

Mummy said goodbye and left me there. The children were wild and I didn't know them so when no one was looking I ran out of the room and out of the building and back to our house.

When Mummy saw me she put me on her lap and spanked me. I cried so hard I began to choke and Mummy had to bring me water. She said I mustn't cross the street alone ever again. I don't know why. I can see if there's a car. It's not as if Mummy can see and I can't see. We both see the same.

If Daddy knew Mummy hit me he'd be angry. But I never told him.

First Day of School

Dori

When I wake up I need Desitin on my jinnie. Shoshana puts it on. For some reason she isn't angry this morning. She's being nice to me.

We make our bed and have breakfast. Breakfast is always the same—bread and jam and either oatmeal or semolina or eggs or wheat puffs and milk.

Any egg is fine with me as long as it's not soft-boiled. I'd rather die than eat the white of a soft-boiled egg. I don't mind scrambled or omelette or fried or hard-boiled mashed with margarine. For fried I don't mind if the yellow is soft. I just don't like when the white is soft. The white is a whole different story.

After breakfast an adult comes to talk to us about Passover. She tells us the story of Moses freeing the slaves. Everyone has to be equal. No one's allowed to make another person a slave. We sing—

> *Sweet spring*
> *Sweet spring*
> *Passover*
> *You bring*

Not a very interesting song. Not a very good tune either. Then we sing—

> *We were slaves*
> *And now and now and now and now*
> *And now we're free*

That one's better because you can shout it. Then we sing about Eliyahu the Grape.[28] I guess he's the person in charge of the grapes. And then we learn a new song in Aramaic *dezabenababitreizuzei* and we all start laughing and getting wild so the adult tells us to draw pictures of spring to decorate the Dining Hall. We draw some pictures and run outside to play.

Our First Year

21 January 1949. The blowing up of the mosque has had its effect on us. No one views the incident with other than mixed feelings, but the army and the government were insistent and needless to say they have the last word. After innumerable considerations involving the significance of destroying this chief building and symbol of the village, most of us agree now that it had to be done. It would have been a useless gesture to preserve this symbol of a population that showed itself to be, when one views the thing factually and unsentimentally, our hardened enemies whom we have no intention of permitting to return.

The whole appearance of the village has undergone a transformation. It's now a mass of ruins, and yet most of us agree it's better this way. The hovels, the filth, the medieval atmosphere— it's gone now, for the most part. Bring on the bulldozers and let's plant trees!

Dori

I climb the monkey bars outside the Children's House. I used to be afraid to hang with only my legs but now I can. Daddy helped me. He held my legs and when I was ready I told him to let go. It was easy in the end.

The sky is beautiful and blue. Everyone is playing tag. I like it alone on top of the monkey bars. I can see everything. I'm going to be a writer and that means I need to see things. I need to see what people are doing and figure out what they are thinking.

I see my brother David going somewhere with his friends Noam and Amnoni. They're going in the direction of the carpentry shop. I know what they're thinking. They're thinking about how much fun they're going to have.

A Good Vantage Point

Dori

Lulu runs over and climbs halfway up the monkey bars to tell me something. Her father is going on a special trip to Gush Halav after lunch and we're allowed to come with him. Only a few children are allowed. My brother David and Noam and Amnoni are coming too. Noam is Lulu's brother. We all have to meet at the chicken coop after lunch.

Gush Halav is an Arab village. It's called Jish in Arabic. So far I've only seen it from the road.

Lunch takes a long time. The tomatoes are mushy and the cucumbers are bitter.[29] I put a slice of tomato on my head. Lulu laughs and puts a slice of cucumber on her head. Someone else is giving us lunch today so we can do whatever we want.

Dessert is bread and jam. We don't want to be late so we fold the bread and eat it on the way out. Then we run down to the chicken coop.

Baby Diary

July 10
For three days she had five feedings. But each time I got up at 4:00 to feed her. I took her outside for the first time and the next day I gave her her first bath. She responded nicely and lay comfortably and quietly in the tub.

And then I took her for a walk. Every day after the third feeding at around 5:00 she wakes up. I give her water and wait another hour for food. She has a rash on her face. I'm worried.

Dori

Well here we are in Gush Halav. Or Jish. We're sitting on two benches in the back of a truck. The back of the truck doesn't have a roof. It was windy riding here even though there's no wind when you stand still.

An old Arab man comes over to our truck and gives us a honeycomb. He's very smiley and excited. We take the honeycomb which makes the man even more smiley and excited. There isn't much honey on it but it's fun to suck.

Lulu's father goes away to talk to someone. The houses in Jish look poor. The windows don't have glass or screens so I don't know how they keep the bugs out. There's a pretty well on one side and a donkey tied to a tree. I like wells.

David says *they don't even have bathrooms*. He says *they have to go in holes in the ground*.

I say *I don't believe you*.

Some children with bare feet come over to look at us. I wish I had something to give them. I feel like the ostriches who forgot to bring their presents.

Jascala

~

ADDRESS: Town of Jish   PRICE RANGE: Reasonable
PHONE: 04/698-7762   CUISINE: Local
RATING: 5/5   UPDATED: 2011

REVIEW—Apart from the typical but memorable hummus, the menu includes original Lebanese salads (including the not-to-be-missed fattoush, a bread salad), an array of fried pastries served with piquant yogurt sauce, and vegetarian stuffed vine leaves. Hot dishes include mushroom dumplings served with side dishes of delicately fried rice. The fare is scrumptious all round. The generous salads, made with fresh chard, dill and wild mallow, are exceptional, and many of the dishes are family recipes made by the owner's mother.

SEATS: 150. CREDIT CARDS: DC, AE, MC, V

Dori

We're back from Gush Halav. I'm having a fight with my brother David. He calls me *zonah* and I call him *zoneh* and he laughs and says there's no such thing as *zoneh*.[30] I don't care.

It's because he wouldn't read me the joke that came with his Bazooka bubble gum. He wouldn't even let me look at it. He kept it all to himself and laughed at me because I was begging.

The only reason I like Bazooka bubble gum is the wrapper with the jokes. I like the pictures and the way the paper feels and smells. And the jokes of course.

I find Lulu and we sit under the stairs that go up to her parents' Room. That's where we sit when Lulu gets her little round box of candies on Friday.

Lulu says *my father is a calboy*. I ask *what's a calboy* and she says *someone who looks after horses and wears a calboy hat*. I say *my father cooks for the whole kibbutz*. Lulu kisses me on my cheek and I kiss her back on her cheek and she kisses me and then I kiss her and we laugh until our stomachs hurt.

Thy Neck with Chains of Gold

MARINA   You're sure you don't have anything more to tell us?

MICHAEL   No, I think that's it.

MARINA   So, with your permission, I'll go look at your son. He's sick, in case you forgot.

MICHAEL   How is he?

MARINA   You can get the details *(as she slams the door)* from his Minder! *(Exits the room. On the porch MARINA puts on her boots and exits)*

MICHAEL   *(to RICKY)* Did I say something wrong?

RICKY   Did you say something *right*?

MICHAEL   Well, I'd better look in on Effie.

RICKY   Good idea.

MICHAEL   *(to RITA)* There's dancing tonight …

RICKY   She's tired.

RITA   *(to RICKY)* Thank you. It's nice to have a spokesperson. Saves my breath.

RICKY   Always glad to be of help.
          (MICHAEL puts bottle of Arak on table)

RICKY   Where did you get that?

MICHAEL   Some of my best friends are Arabs.

RICKY   When the ravens fed Elijah in the desert and he had visions—it must have been Arabs giving him arak. You see, "orev", raven, and "arav", Arab, have a common root. *(Gives MICHAEL a hard sock on the arm)* Thanks, pal. *(Returns to his writing)*

MICHAEL   *(holding his arm)* What's this all about?

RITA   A bird project.

MICHAEL *(rubbing his arm)* I don't know anything about birds.
RICKY Rita does.
RITA Since when?
RICKY When she dances she seems to fly—from one nest into the other.

Dori

On Passover there's going to be a big celebration with parents and children. I love holidays.

In Canada Daddy was the leader of Camp Bilu'im. It was a summer camp for big people only and it really was fun, just like its name.[31] Once when it was already dark everyone walked in a long long line to a huge campfire and while we walked we sang—

> When Moses was in Egyptland
> Let my people go
> Oh pressed so hard they could not stand
> Let my people go
> Go down Moses! Waaay down in Egyptland!
> Tell old Pharoah. To let my people go.[32]

Daddy carried me on his shoulders in the dark. We walked slowly because it's important to remember slaves. I'm never going to forget that walk. I'm never going to forget anything.

I like the Moses song but the Joshua song is even better—

> Joshua fought the battle of Jericho Jericho Jericho
> Joshua fought the battle of Jericho
> And the walls came a tumbling down
> Well you can talk about the battle of Gideon!
> You can talk about the battle of Saul!
> But there's none like good old Joshua
> At the battle of Jericho. That morning!

We had a record with both those songs on Davaar Street.
They're both beautiful but the Joshua one hurts my heart.

Leonora/Lolo/Leah Previn
(1927–1959)

Older sister of André Previn;

worked with the poor of Los Angeles in her early twenties;

immigrated to Israel;

joined the founders of Eldar in 1949;

changed name to Leah;

invited Isaac Stern to visit Eldar before a scheduled concert in
    Haifa;

Leah remembered by Isaac as beautiful;

Eldar remembered as a military observation post;

members' harsh living conditions and evident love of music
    prompted Isaac, with characteristic generosity, to issue an invi-
    tation to his concert at no charge;

concert was sold out;

Isaac refused to perform unless seats were found for the forty
    Eldar members who showed up;

barrels and crates set up for them in wings;

Leah is remembered by all who knew her as kind and gentle;

Naftali changed his name from Stavitsky to Satie in the hope of
    impressing her;

ploy failed;

at some point Leah returned to the United States;

was diagnosed with cancer at age thirty-two;

told André but not her parents;

died four days after André won an Academy Award;

André in New York at the time, working on a television special;

André told his biographer that he and Lolo were close though in
    many ways opposites;

photos of her are not included in Previn biographies/memoirs; details of her life are now known only to those who knew her personally.

Dori

It's the middle of the night and Skye is crying. Skye hardly ever cries but she's sick. I say *call the Night Guard* but she doesn't want to. I'm surprised. Skye is exactly the sort of person to call the Guard.

I decide to do it myself. I like being the one who gets up and calls the Guard. It means I'm big now and I can help.

I walk over to the loudspeaker on the wall and shout up *Skye is sick!*

I hear a voice coming out of the loudspeaker but it's full of noise. I shout again *Skye is sick!* and the voice comes out again but I still can't hear it.

There's nothing more I can do. I go back to bed. I tell Skye *I called the Night Guard.* She isn't crying as much now. She's waiting for the Guard.

II
The World Below

Will it be a king or a non-king
Who establishes a territory of
dominion in the world below?
—UGARITIC BAAL CYCLE, C. 1300 BCE

Dori

I'm on my way to the Room when I see a game on the lawn. The bigger children are playing army. They're using sticks for pretend rifles. A boy I don't know is the commander.

I find a rifle and join the game. We do left right left attention at ease salute. I don't really understand left right left. Everyone walks left right left. There's no other way to walk.

A boy grabs my rifle. I don't bother fighting over it. It's not worth the trouble. Anyhow the game is boring. The commander is doing the same thing over and over.

I run to the Room and show Daddy attention at ease salute. He doesn't like it. He doesn't like the whole army business. I ask him *did you fight in the army?* and he says *not exactly.* He doesn't want to tell me. There was something else I had to ask him but I forget.

Our First Year

23 January 1949. We are now living in dispersed areas in the few good buildings that were left standing in the village. Living quarters assigned of course in conformity with needs of security. A spooky and unpleasant process to stumble home in the dark and rainy night, with a glaring battery light and all sorts of looming and unfamiliar ruins seeming to crowd forward on every side.

Some of us still get lost from time to time on the unfamiliar paths, complicated terraces and treacherous rubble. I often feel like something from one of those Kafkaesque novels when I step out of my damp room filled with smoke (can't get the fireplace to burn properly) and walk over the huge white stones, past the half-destroyed wall, and watch a wild cat come running out of the small building with the caved-in roof.

Dori

There's a song my brother David likes to sing with his friends. It's about the legend of the Red Rock. The legend says that there's a place beyond the mountains called the Red Rock and no one who goes there returns alive. Three lads decide to go anyhow. All they take with them is an old dream and a map and a canteen. What I like best about the song is that after each part you get to say *oh the Red Rock, the Red Rock.*[33]

I don't know the whole song but in the end the lads die. I asked Daddy why everyone who goes to the Red Rock dies but he didn't want to tell me. The question made him angry. Not at me though. At something else.

I kept asking and asking and finally he said *because it's dangerous.* I asked *what can happen?* but he only said *it's not safe* because he didn't want to tell me but he didn't want to lie. I asked *if people know they're going to die, why do they go?* and he said *because it's so beautiful.*

That doesn't make sense in my opinion. What's the point of seeing something beautiful if you die the minute you see it?

David says Ben Gurion won't let the radio play the song about the Red Rock because it might give people the idea to go there. But the lad in the song dies so how would that make someone want to go? Also if Ben Gurion is afraid people will go to the Red Rock, is it a legend or is it real?

I don't understand this whole Red Rock business.

Petra

Archaeological city in Jordan;

capital of the Nabataeans in the sixth century BCE;

chosen by the BBC as one of forty places to see before you die;

unknown in the West before 1812;

in May 1953 two young Israeli hikers challenged themselves to reach Petra and succeeded, travelling mostly by night, hiding from armed Bedouins, scaling walls of rock, crossing streams, bypassing waterfalls, climbing and descending cliffs and ravines, avoiding goat herds;

their success encouraged Eitan Mintz, Yaakov Kleifeld, Gila Ben-Akiva, Arik Magar and nursing graduate Miriam Monderer (pictured resting above) who attempted the journey in August but, possibly following a snakebite, approached the police station for help, were presumably taken for aggressors and shot;

their bodies were returned to Israel the next day;

three years later, in April 1956, paratroopers Dror Levi and Dimitri Berman made the attempt and were shot, though Berman managed to haul himself home;[34]

a year later Menahem Ben-David, Ram Pragai, Kalman Shlafsky and Dan Gilad were killed on the way to Petra;

song about Petra fatalities banned 30 July 1958;

trips to Petra safe for Israelis since the 1994 peace agreement with Jordan;

one-day group tours from Eilat available for $200 per adult.

Dori

My brother David found a jug somewhere. Exactly like the fairy's jugs in *Pinocchio*.

I get very excited. David lets me hold the jug and I try to put it on my head but the handle is too high.

I look inside and suddenly a horrible smell comes out of the jug. The worst smell I ever smelled in my whole life. I make a face and a sound like throwing up and David laughs.

The jugs looked so nice in *Pinocchio* and on the heads of the Arab women and I really wanted one. Now I don't even know if I like jugs any more.

Our First Year

29 January 1949. Cold and cloudy once again; we're preparing for another bout of rain. Practically not a drop of water on the kibbutz, not even enough to take care of the cooking. Something must be wrong with the army truck.

Meanwhile we're working full speed to repair some of the buildings. Guard duty very uneventful, much to our relief, and we don't even hear shots. The army pulled out completely a number of days ago, and they only come around now to discuss our defences.

Dori

I'm on my way to the Room when I see the man from the ruins. He always wears a long dark coat. Even in summer. My brother David says his name is either Jeremiah ben-Jacob or Arnold and he sleeps on straw with the wild dogs.

I decide to follow him. I want to see those ruins.

But as soon as I get there he pushes me down on the ground with his hand and opens his coat. He's naked inside the coat and his skin is very white. I scream and run away as fast as I can.

I'm still interested in the ruins though. I'll ask David and Noam and Amnoni to take me with them next time they go.

Thy Neck with Chains of Gold

RITA, *alone in her room, moves to the wall separating her room from* MICHAEL *and* MARINA's, *and knocks. She waits for a response. The knock is returned. She sits and waits for the door to open. Enter* MICHAEL.

MICHAEL   What's a nice girl like you doing on a tropical island like this?

RITA   I'm waiting for my lover. He'll sail in on the tide, just when the sun sets along the pink horizon.

MICHAEL   Haven't we met before? Yes, I remember. I see you often in my dreams, living in the Middle East, where the cannons roar and the wind howls and the rain falls incessantly on tin rooftops.

RITA   Hark! My lover approacheth …

MICHAEL   What kind of man is he?

RITA   Tall and handsome—and terribly vain. When he looks at me, I tremble.

Dori

There's a beautiful lullaby—

> *Lullaby the ship is sailing*
> *Lullaby the waves are rocking*
> *Moon o moon*
> *The ship starts to sway*
> *Lullaby lullay*
> *Let your song fade away*

Lullaby three birds left the bay
Lullaby one froze on the way
Moon o moon
The second was shot
And the very last one
Lullaby lullay
Your name forgot

Mummy says the song is about Jews coming to Palestina. That's what Israel was called before it was ours. Palestina. I like that word. *Nina from Palestina.*

Mummy explains that the birds are symbols. Some Jews died on the way to Palestina and some were killed by the Enemy and some forgot they were Jews. I love symbols.

I have a question though. If a third were killed and a third died and a third forgot they were Jews then who was left to come to Palestina? That song is not exactly right because here we are.

Our First Year

1 February 1949. Not rain, but snow, snow! Twelve inches deep in places and still falling. The whole appearance of the place is transformed. The ruins of the village look like reclining polar bears and the terraces and familiar paths are hidden. The pipes are frozen and a few people have twisted their ankles in bad falls. We're still trying to repair buildings, but it's almost impossible to work in the snow. The carpentry shop is working full blast.

Dori

I ask Daddy to read *The Little Matchgirl* to me. He laughs and says *but it makes you cry.* But I keep asking and in the end he gives in. I don't mind crying.

When he gets to the fourth match I begin to cry. The girl sees her dead grandmother and wants to go with her. And in the morning they find the little girl frozen in the snow with the matches in her hand. I want a different ending and I cry and cry.

Daddy laughs and says *I told you it would make you cry.* He gives me a big white handkerchief to blow my nose. I say *make up a different ending* and he tries but it doesn't work because I know it's not the real ending.

Then he says *after Passover I'll bring you a surprise from the city* and that makes my crying stop. I love that word—*surprise.* I wonder what it will be. I'm not really allowed to have anything that's just mine but if Daddy buys it for me it isn't my fault.

Baby Diary

July 12
The rash is worse. It's spread to her entire face. I put on cod liver oil. Today she really smiled at me when I spoke to her.

Dori

It's Passover today. Shoshana brings us white shirts and clean shorts. I'm hoping she'll give me shorts with a big zipper on the side and she does.

We go to the fields with all the children and all the adults. There's a tractor decorated with flowers and the bigger children sing in a choir. Some people get up and dance to Stalks in the Field. Someone reads a poem about figs. Everyone is happy.

Daddy is sitting on the ground smiling. I sit on his lap. There's a speech about peace with the Arabs. I remember what I wanted to ask Daddy. It's about the toilets in Gush

Halav. But he wants to hear the speech so he whispers *tell me after.*

Suddenly it's way past suppertime and the adults have to go to the Dining Hall to read the Haggada[35] and eat and we have to go to the Children's House. At least we were together almost the whole day.

Poem About Figs

Lo, the winter is past, the rain is over and gone
The flowers appear on the earth
The time of the singing of birds is come
And the voice of the turtledove is heard in our
    land
The fig tree puts forth its green figs
And the vines are in blossom; they give forth
    their fragrance
Arise, my love, my fair one, and come away
My dove is in the clefts of the rock
In the secret places of the hills
Let me see thy face
Let me hear thy voice
For sweet is thy voice
And thy face is comely
Take us the foxes, the little foxes
That spoil the vineyards
For our vineyards are in blossom
My beloved is mine and I am his
He feedeth among the lilies
Until the sun spreads, and the shadows flee away
Turn my beloved
And be thou like a roe or a young hart
Upon the distant mountains.

Dori

Marx is famous for saying *share everything*. I don't know why that made him famous. Everyone already knows it's more fair if you share.

I remember to ask Daddy about the toilets in Gush Halav. I say *David says they go in holes in the ground*. Daddy really really doesn't want to talk about this topic. He says *I don't know* but how can that be? I say *but do they have toilets?* and he says *they don't have plumbing like we have*.

I say *why don't we give them half our toilets?* For example we have two toilets in the Children's House. We could give one to Jish.

He says *our country doesn't have enough money right now but as soon as we have more everyone will have plumbing*. I ask *how can we get more money* and he says *we have to work hard*.

I'm glad I'm only a child. I don't want to work all day. I might be a little bit lazy. Shoshana likes to sing that song to us when she wakes us up in the morning—

> *Get up lazybones*
> *And off you go to work*
> *Get up lazybones*
> *And off you go to work*
> *Cuku-Riku Cuku-Riku*
> *Hear the rooster crow*
> *Cuku-Riku Cuku-Riku*
> *Hear the rooster crow*

in that mean laughing voice of hers. If Shoshana thinks it's bad to be lazy it can't be that bad.

Our First Year

3 February 1949. The snow is beginning to melt and living conditions are really tough. Just to get in and out of bed, to keep clean, to drain the water out of the room, to shuffle from one meal to the next, to say nothing of putting in an eight- or nine-hour work day—in other words, just to go through the simple process of keeping alive during the twenty-four hour day saps all of one's energy.

Cultural activities are almost impossible, but we try, we try. Now preparing a skit for the celebration when the folks from Kibbutz Shaar Hagolan arrive. Those of us who used to whine that the days of pioneering are over in Israel have stopped whining.

Dori

I'm in love with Tarzan. There was a movie about him today and now I love him. He's the handsomest man in the world. Until now Daddy was the handsomest but now it's Tarzan and Daddy together.

Daddy tells me more about Tarzan. How his parents died in an airplane crash in the jungle and the apes raised him. That's why he knows the language of apes and other animals.

A funny song about God comes on the radio. In Canada they actually believe in God but we're more advanced here. Daddy really likes this song. It makes him laugh.

> *God was simply feeling bored as hell one day*
> *He thought hey say*
> *Why not create a world out of clay*
> *But how much better*
> *How much better it would be*
> *For every animal and tree*
> *If instead of all this muddle*
> *He'd gone and solved*
> *A crossword puzzle*

The song has a lot of the crazy things humans do. When it's over Daddy sings the lines he remembers and laughs some more. He's happy here in Eldar.

Between the Motion and the Act

A beautiful American woman was standing outside the hotel with a huge knapsack on her back, waiting for a bus. Nat was trying to think of a way to offer her his services when she recognized him—a few months ago she'd appeared in the YG Federation office in Tel Aviv to ask about visiting a kibbutz. He had been there by chance and they had talked. Her name, she said, was Joy.

He'd stared at her smooth shiny black hair falling gently on her soft shoulders and framing the white smooth neck that extended from her summer dress. He'd boldly looked at her red lips, high cheekbones, perfect Nordic nose, and bright grey eyes. How could her parents have guessed that she'd become the embodiment of her name?

"Why don't you come to our kibbutz?" he'd offered and was aware of the blood flowing in his reproductive veins.

"I want a kibbutz of Hebrew speakers," she'd said, mentioning a few near the Syrian border.

"Are you busy tonight?"

"Yes, but maybe another time."

But Joy didn't vanish forever; here she was now in Haifa. And she remembered him!

"Do you have a place to stay here in Haifa?" His thoughts worked quickly with the acumen of a wolf.

"Yes, the kibbutz I'm on has a house on the Carmel."

"Are you free tonight?" he asked, remembering the last time he was rejected.

"Yes." She smiled and he carried her heavy knapsack. He was very happy. He seated her in a café and asked her to wait ten minutes so he could put on clean clothes and tell Rubin about his change of plans. He hurried up the stairs. Rubin lay on his bed in underwear and undershirt and read the Palestine Post while waving away the flies with his other hand.

"Rubin, I have a fabulous girl waiting for me. If you want to come with us, hurry."

He didn't even raise his eyes from the newspaper. "Ha ha," he said.

"Okay," Nat said, trying to hide his relief. "You don't have to come."

He hurried to shower. He couldn't find the leg of his pants as he raised them from the dusty floor. Rubin started to notice that something was up. He lay down the newspaper and leaned on his elbow in amusement. He saw that Nat wasn't joking, grabbed his clothes, applied Brylcreem to his wild curls and ran after Nat, buttoning his pants and shouting, "Wait for me, wait a minute!"

Nat introduced Rubin to Joy. Rubin gave an amazed look, as if to say, Where the hell did you manage to find such a charming creature? Her face was like pale petals surrounded by black hair, her exposed legs were lovely, her full body rustled under her thin summer dress, radiating naughty adventures.

They walked along the neat streets lined with trees and decided on supper at the Balfour Cellar. Leo the barman played favourite oldies like Frankie Laine crooning "Jezebel."

They questioned her. She had come to Israel because her parents were Quakers and she was interested in peace, she told them.

"You want to help the Arabs, no?" Rubin was agitated, chewing his liver with an open mouth and unabashed enthusiasm.

A ghostly shadow passed for a moment in her eyes.

"We don't make any distinctions in providing our services," she said. "The kibbutzim interest me as a way of life, as a way of achieving harmony on the basis of mutual help." She cut her portion with deliberation and delicacy, like a girl from a good home.

As she munched on her french fries in the murky basement, she began to shower them with questions. What sort of work do they do? What are their roles apart from their regular workday? How many are they? How far are they from the border?

Nat tried to stifle his suspicious nature. His answers were measured, but Rubin, who had already managed to drink a few glasses of whiskey, and who was also drunk on Joy's stunning beauty, spoke freely. In any case, he always jokingly claimed that any information extracted from them was completely useless to anyone. Maybe he was right. From the minute that she learned he was in charge of "security", that he was a former Air Force Pilot who'd received a Silver Star, her eyes and ears were tuned only to him.

Rubin and Nat worriedly split the bill. When they emerged from the basement bar to the street, which glowed with neon lights, a few army officers greeted her. She left her companions for a few seconds, and had a quiet exchange with her military acquaintances. Rubin and Nat, themselves former soldiers, mused again on the attractions that beautiful girls exert on high-ranking military men.

She sat between them at a movie, laughed out loud, and licked a popsicle with her scarlet tongue. She thanked them from the bottom of her heart and refused to let them accompany her home.

The two disappointed friends took the bus back to their paltry room.

A few months later, two policemen arrived at the kibbutz and asked whether anyone there had seen a girl named Joy. Nat happened to be at the office at that moment. "I know her," he said.

"So where is she?" asked the police officer.

"I don't know."

"How do you know her?"

Nat told him and then asked, "Why are you looking for her?"

They explained that she'd been under surveillance for quite some time, on suspicion of espionage. They had lost her, though, they said. She was last seen boarding a bus and had probably crossed the border by now, or escaped on a ship from Acre.

Dori

Daddy bought me a book about Tarzan! He found it in the city!

The book doesn't have a lot of pictures but it's full of stories about Tarzan King of the Apes. Daddy's going to read me the stories. I love Tarzan so much.

Tarzan in the Middle East

Eleven Tarzan books were translated into Hebrew in the 1930s;
Tarzan became a national obsession in the 1950s;
by 1961, ten Tarzan series were being published without copyright in Israel;
a total of over 900 issues were printed;
in some stories Tarzan helped illegal Jewish immigration to Mandated Palestine, for which he was imprisoned by the British;
in others he singlehandedly broke the Egyptian blockade at Suez, killing many Egyptian soldiers along the way;
in one series Tarzan is dead but an Israeli named Dan-Tarzan crashes in the jungle and is reared by a descendent of Kala the ape;
Dan-Tarzan becomes a Mossad agent;
captures former Nazis;
finds lost city of ancient Hebrew warriors.
In parallel developments in Syria and Lebanon, Tarzan successfully battled Jews.

Dori

Today is Gilead's birthday. He's turning six. I don't know if Gilead has any parents here on Eldar. He wasn't born here but he calls someone here *Mummy* and someone else *Daddy* so I don't know what the story is.

For his birthday there's a movie in one of the Rooms. The wall is the screen. It's so crowded there's hardly any room to sit. A lot of children from different Groups want to see the movie. It's *Hansel and Gretel*.

I'm a bit scared when the witch puts Hansel in a cage. Gilead holds my hand. It's the first time I'm holding a child's hand to be less scared. That means something but I'm not sure what.

Our First Year

5 February 1949. Another day without bread. Some time in the future, when we have a chance to relax, and these days are no more than fond, rugged memories, perhaps someone will sit down and write the story of what we will call the Saga of Bread. Our bread comes from Safed, something like 27 kilometres away, which means, since we have no transportation, that a team of our boys has to set out every other day or so, by hitch-hiking or by walking, to pick it up.

Sometimes they get a ride, sometimes they don't. To tramp up and down these hills with a heavy sack of bread on one's shoulders, in rain or hail or snow, is no joke, and since I've never done it myself, being a mere woman, I'm not competent to describe the intensity of the experience.

This week, Amos came home so weatherbeaten and exhausted from the trip that he couldn't drag the bread up the hill the last 500 metres, and he was in bed for two days after the trek.

Dori

Shoshana is in a bad mood again. Lulu and Elan have to soak their tushies in a pail of water because they have itchy spots. They're not allowed to scratch because scratching makes it worse. But it's like when you have a mosquito bite—you just can't help scratching.

But it seems Shoshana caught Elan scratching.

She grabs two rags from the rag-bag and then she grabs Elan and throws him on a bed. Gilead's bed. She makes us all come with her. She ties Elan's wrists to the metal part of the bed so he won't scratch. We all have to stand next to the bed and watch and laugh. We're not laughing but Shoshana pretends we are.

Elan has the scared smile. His wrists are skinny and he shivers. Shoshana screams *you see what I have to do you see what you make me do!*

I'm going to tell Daddy. He'll have to believe me this time.[36]

Theories of Education[37]

We all understood from the start that educating our children properly was the single most important facet of the kibbutz project. In order to create a society dedicated to principles of justice, equality and humanity, we had to ensure that our children received the best possible education.

In pursuit of this goal, I began my work in 1911. At that time I became acquainted with two books: in Hebrew, *Psychological Discussions for Teachers,* and in German, *Aus der Praxis der Arbeitsschule* by Pabst. Two volumes of *The Free School,* in Russian, also came into my hands. One article, 'Independent work and the joy of creativity' captivated me, opening up before me new philosophical vistas. Two years later I went to study in Germany and Switzerland. For a whole year I waited in Leipzig for the summer course in methodology of activity orientation. I read everything I could find on general psychology and progressive teaching for ten to twelve hours a day—Gaudig, Ley and others. One book that impressed me was Dewey's *The School and Society,* although not all his methods attracted me. In 1921, two extremely impressive studies reached me. One was the work of S. Schatzky, *Brand New Life,* and the other was by Bernfeld, on Baumgarten's experience.

After reading Bernfeld, and more importantly, after living with young children at the school in Tel Aviv, I underwent a revolution. I gave up experimental psychology and threw myself into the study of psychoanalysis. Much later on I came into possession of the studies of A.S. Neill. I read them all with the utmost enjoyment.

Dori

I dreamed God was a giant who could skip over mountains with a single step. My brother David was holding his left hand and I was holding his right hand and we leaped over the mountains with him.

Finally we reached some ruins in Yehupitz. That was where God lived. There was a round floor made of smooth white stone and old stone columns all around. Some of the columns were broken because they were so old.[38] I had to go to the toilet but there wasn't any toilet paper so God gave me two rocks instead. Rocks! How can I wipe with rocks? But I didn't say anything because that's all God had.

Yehupitz isn't a real place. It's just something you say when you don't have an answer. Like when I ask Daddy where Mummy is he says *Yehupitz* and laughs.

In my dream God looked a little like the Friendly Giant from television. I loved that show. Especially the beginning with the beautiful tune and the little chairs in the castle. You could choose the little chair or a rocking chair or a chair for two to curl up in.

I don't know which chair I would choose. I think the chair for two to curl up in. Maybe on different days I could sit in different chairs.

The reason we don't have television here is the same reason we don't have makeup or made-up hair. Pioneers don't get fooled so easily.

One time in Canada Mummy took me to a department store and all of a sudden she said *can you keep a secret Dori?* And I said *yes*. And she said *you have to promise never ever ever to tell anyone.* I said *I promise.* Usually I'm not good at keeping secrets but I decided to keep this one no matter what. She said *I'm going to try on that makeup.* There were two women dressed like nurses putting makeup on for free. Mummy said *I want to see what it feels like to be a real woman.* Even I knew that was a silly thing to say.

Mummy sat in a chair and the two women put makeup on her face. I sat next to one of the mannequins and looked at the perfume bottles. Some were blue but most were plain glass. I love little bottles.

When the two women finished Mummy said *thank you* and we went to the bathroom. She tried to wash everything off but it wasn't easy. Some of the makeup was stuck on. Mummy said *they put on way too much—I look like I'm wearing a mask.*

I never told anyone our secret and I never will as long as I live.

Thy Neck with Chains of Gold

ELI *knocks on* RITA's *door and enters without waiting for a reply. He is preoccupied. He carries a radio and his work assignment board.*

ELI   I can't finish the work assignments in the office. Everyone comes in and gives me arguments. May I …

RITA   Of course.

ELI   The radio's for you. It's your turn this week.

RITA   Are you sure?

ELI   That's what the Members' Committee told me.

RITA   Thanks, Eli.

ELI   *(manipulating the cards on the board as he speaks)* Deena wants two work days in the laundry. She'll get one because Dudi has to tie grape vines. There'll be carpentry tomorrow—Shmulik will spray the orchard. Marina in sanitation—no, I promised her shabat. Jonah—chickens. Morty will deliver the laundry and kerosene to the nurseries and then he'll help in the garage. Benjamin, store-house. Sammy—sheep. Ricky will clear rocks from field number 6 along with Tova, no—she's sick. The three Danish kids can help him. What'll I do with Peretz? Two left hands, three left feet … let him continue in the library. And Paula mending and ironing and that's it.

RITA You couldn't let me have a few hours' help tomorrow, could you?

ELI I'm afraid not. We have five extra people on guard tonight. *(Looks at chart, then at her)* Well … Paula doesn't have to iron all day.

RITA *(hugs him)* Thank you, Eli.

ELI *(to MICHAEL)* You'd better look at this—you're not driving for a couple of days. Marina told me it's too hard on her.

MICHAEL Oh she did, did she?

ELI I put you down for work on the kibbutz until Effie's well.

MICHAEL This is ridiculous.

ELI Marina's falling off her feet. She can't work properly.

MICHAEL So you're concerned with her work, not with the kid.

ELI The child is the educational committee's concern. *(looks at RITA)*

RITA Effie would be very happy—if his father were home sometimes.

ELI So Moishi will drive.

(RITA turns on the radio)

MICHAEL But I'm the driver!

ELI Maybe I'll take you off the road for good. Some people think you ought to work on the farm for a change.

MICHAEL I work more hours than anyone on this kibbutz! Last week I spent three days chasing around for building materials which we didn't have money to buy. I also finagled all that feed for the sheep. I swiped two broken army jeeps and Matty fixed them up so they're good

	as new. I'm not only the best driver around here, I also have initiative, and you know it.
	(The radio plays instrumental rock and roll music.)
ELI	Please change the station.
MICHAEL	This music too bourgeois for you?
RITA	Sure, Eli.
MICHAEL	So where did you put me? *(Finding his work card on the board)* In the kitchen!
ELI	That's right. Early shift.
	(MICHAEL curses under his breath)
MICHAEL	Let me drive the tractor tomorrow.
RITA	Just like the kids. Anything on wheels.
ELI	Be thankful I didn't put you on guard duty. The army found a mine and tracks that led across the border …
MICHAEL	I'll guard all night.
ELI	It's not necessary. We need you in the kitchen—at 4:30 a.m.
MICHAEL	Yes, Boss.
ELI	Don't call me Boss.
MICHAEL	Sorry, Boss.
RITA	I'll make you some coffee, Eli. You'd better put on *gatkes* or you'll freeze on guard tonight.
MICHAEL	*Gatkes!* What are we, decrepit?
RITA	It has nothing to do with being decrepit.
ELI	Actually, I think I have a little rheumatism.
MICHAEL	There, what did I tell you?
ELI	*(to RITA)* You've been Michael's neighbour for years. How do you tolerate him?
RITA	I'm very good with problem children. *(She is about to give ELI his coffee but MICHAEL takes it out of her hands)* What are you doing?
MICHAEL	He won't drink this capitalist brew. This coffee was ground by an international imperialist monopoly.
RITA	*(takes cup)* Oh, shut up.
MICHAEL	Where have all our principles gone to?

Dori

I tell Daddy about Elan. I lie on the floor of the Room and I put my arms out to show him.

Daddy doesn't say anything. I don't understand. If he believes me why doesn't he do something? And if he doesn't believe me why doesn't he believe me?

I did cheat once in War. Daddy knew I was cheating. I gave myself all the good cards. Daddy asked *did you take all the good cards for yourself*? and I said *no* and then a few cards later he asked again and I said *no* again but he knew I was lying because it's too much of a coincidence for one person to get all the kings and queens and jacks. But it was only a game.

And he doesn't know about the time I pinched Sara's foot.

By the way, it isn't fun playing War if you give yourself all the good cards. You know you're going to win and then you win.

Age of Innocence

Dori

I am really in love with Tarzan.

Transcript of Education Committee Meeting
May 1961

Chair: Coco
Present: Shoshana, Doreet, Edna, Varda, Amos, Martin

Coco: Since the problem with Muki's bedwetting solved itself, Varda would like to bring up the subject of reading to children at bedtime.

Varda: Yes, thank you. I noticed that some Minders don't read to the younger children at all. At every teachers' conference I've been to there's been a huge emphasis on reading out loud. And the children absolutely love it.

Amos: I have "Reading to Children" in my index, if anyone wants to look up articles.

Coco: Your wonderful index! Thank you for keeping that up, Amos.

Varda: Yes, thank you, Amos. I know when I was a Minder I used to read to the children at least an hour a day, usually more. That doesn't include songs and poetry. And now that I'm teaching it hasn't changed. If anything, I read to them even more. Storytime is the children's favourite activity, they always beg for more. We've almost finished *Gulliver's Travels.*

Edna: Don't forget that parents also read to their children during Visits.

Varda: Not all parents have the time, the energy, the inclination or even the Hebrew reading skills.

Martin: Yes, Schopenhauer in Hebrew is quite a challenge.

Varda: What do you think, Doreet?

Doreet: We just had a shipment of new books for little ones—it arrived on Sunday. Some lovely treasures there.

Amos:	Yes, though they all dispersed quite fast into the Diaspora of the Rooms. I think I have a vague notion of who has what ...
Coco:	Let's bring it to a vote. Should we require all Minders to read to children, if possible, starting with the toddlers?

Vote:	For = 7	Against = 0

Shoshana:	I would like to bring up the subject of some children getting tucked in by parents while others are not.
Varda:	We already discussed this and agreed to make exceptions in the case of illness or special situations.
Shoshana:	I'm wondering whether parents alone decide on the special situations or whether the committee decides?
Amos:	We can't call a meeting every time a child has a fever.
Shoshana:	I'm thinking of the special cases that are ongoing.
Martin:	I'm sure no one here would take advantage. We have extraordinary moral fibre in this kibbutz.
Coco:	If there is a specific problem, we can discuss it.
Shoshana:	Everyone knows I'm referring to Dori. It's been five months now, I'm sure she's adjusted.
Coco:	Varda, any comments?
Varda:	Dori spent a year and a half in Canada. She's still having a hard time separating in the evenings.
Amos:	We have to consider how it makes the other children feel. What message it sends out.
Coco:	I don't want to rush things, but the yawns in this room are starting to remind me of "The Lotus Eaters."
Martin:	"There is sweet music here ..."
Varda:	"That softer falls than petals ..."
Coco:	Sorry to move from the sublime to the mundane, but let's vote: Should Varda be allowed to give Dori a goodnight kiss?

Vote:	For = 1	Against = 2	Abstentions = 4

Dori

It's Independence Day. We join a big parade of everyone in Eldar. We hold little Israeli flags that we made and we sit in a gigantic circle and sing songs. Hundreds of songs.

The older children play hide-and-go-seek. I hide behind the barn but no one finds me and when I come back the game is over. Did I win because no one found me or did I lose because I didn't run back without being caught?

The older children go to the clubhouse to dance. We run after them. There's a record of Let's Twist Again Like We Did Last Summer[39] and everyone dances the twist. My brother David is very good at twisting. I love that song. They play it a hundred times. The bigger children don't like the little children getting in the way but we don't care. They keep complaining and we keep getting in their way. They're happy when it's time for us to go back to the Children's House.

I can't wait to be bigger.

Our First Year

14 February 1949. Thirty of us have arrived from the interim kibbutz. It's a cold, rainy, misty drive around the Kinneret, through Safed; the poppies are beautiful, but it was a lousy trip. One has to be in a certain heroic mood to appreciate the transient, vagrant beauties of this country from the back of a truck, in the rain, with inadequate clothing on one's back.

Five of us are housed in a high-ceilinged, stone wall, unplastered room; it leaks, it's damp and oppressive; no windows; a dim lantern provides meagre light; and it's so crowded we'll have to demand that one person move out; there are also a few mice in my corner, but otherwise it's quite comfortable.

In the evening two young Arabs from Jish dropped by and wanted to discuss the political program of the United Workers Party with us. Just like that. They look like intelligent chaps, but it's been very difficult for us to be genuinely interested in politics these past few days.

Dori

My brother David is teaching me how to embroider. The cloth is in a metal circle with a picture in light blue that you follow. Mine is a bird.

David showed me how to do three different stitches. He's very good at embroidering.

In Camp Bilu'im I went to the arts and crafts room every day. The counsellor in that room was very nice. She gave me popsicle sticks and glue and paint and pieces of coloured paper and scissors.

Most scissors don't cut very well it seems. Some don't cut at all. My grandfather in Canada had scissors that were very good at cutting. Why doesn't everyone get that kind?

My grandfather also had a glue bottle with a red rubber top and a crack for the glue to come out. If you squeeze the crack it looks like a mouth opening.

I liked that glue bottle so much that Daddy brought it with him from Canada. Or maybe he found one like it in the city.

At Camp Bilu'im at first I ate with everyone else in the Dining Hall. But then my mother said we had to eat in the kitchen because the campers didn't want little children around.

I didn't want to eat in the kitchen with Sara in her high chair. There wasn't even a table for me. Only a stool and a counter covered with pots and dirty dishes.

I got into a bad mood. I could hear all the campers singing a song about two sisters *she won't do it but her sister will* and having fun. They never even noticed me when I ate with them and if they noticed me they were very nice. I think Mummy made up that story but I don't know why.

Marsha from Arts and Crafts

Dori

By the way I never talked once in that kindergarten Mummy forced me to go to in Canada and I never did anything. I just stood in the corner or sat on a chair and ignored everyone.

The only time I joined in was when they gave us see-through paper to glue behind shapes that you cut out of a black piece of paper. Then on the back it looks messy but in front all you see is the see-through paper shining inside the shapes. That see-through paper was really and truly beautiful. Especially if you held it up to the window. It came in red and blue and yellow and green. I wish we had some here on Eldar.

Wait—there was one other thing. The gold and silver crowns on Purim. I couldn't resist those either.

Our First Year

17 February 1949. Rain-sleet-hail-snow today with breaks of sun and low-hanging, carelessly spun clouds suspended against the hills like artificial cotton clouds.

The team of thirty or so Arabs who were here packing up the abandoned tobacco in the various buildings of the village, under government supervision, have finally left. A very interesting business having them here, especially for those of us who worked with them as half-guard, half-chaperon. Many of them were Christians, good workers, alert, and shrewd, and others were definitely Levantine types concerning whom we have a lot to learn.

One can see at a glance the infernal complicatedness of the Arab question, and here it is, right on our doorstep.

Dori

Here is something I don't think Mummy and Daddy know. My brother David saved my life in Camp Bilu'im. Mummy took me to play on the beach and told me to hold on to the wall of stones if I go into the water. She told David to keep an eye on me.

There wasn't much to do near the wall. I ducked all the way under the water and held my breath and then I came up. Then I ducked again but this time the shirt I was wearing got caught in the wall. I had a shirt on top of my bathing suit because my shoulders were sunburned.

I began to die. The shirt was stuck and I didn't have any air left. I tried to pull the shirt but I couldn't. I can't even say how scared I was.

But David grabbed me and saved my life. He saw that I was stuck and he ran over and saved me. He said *why did you go underwater? Don't go underwater again.*

I told Mummy I drowned but I don't think she heard me. I don't even think David knows he saved my life. No one knows except me.

Odds of a Shirt Getting Caught in a Groyne

He was nearly ten, flailing pale awkward limbs.

Dori

Daddy has *Dr Seuss*! We had those three books in Canada and now here they are in Eldar.

I know all three books by heart. The one with the Cat in the Hat and the snow and the one with the Cat in the Hat and his tricks and *One Fish Two Fish*.

I love everything about those books. From beginning to end. Mummy and Daddy love them too. They laugh when we read them. They read them and I say the words at the same time and then they kiss me.

Dr Seuss has a funny name because he's not a doctor and he's not a horse.[40] His name matches his books.

Our First Year

19 February 1949. The sun has finally come; no rain, a little wind, and huge, high clouds. The waves and layers of hills stretch away in tones of pink, orange and grey. Much washing, reading, taking of walks, bundled-up against the wind, but everyone basking and blinking in the sun. Quiet communion with earth and weather.

Dori

It's my birthday today. I'm six years old. But first there's breakfast and lunch and naptime. I'm so excited I can't sleep.

Finally it's Wake-Up. Mummy does the Wake-Up. She has a garland for my hair but it turns out I don't have a dress. Shoshana was supposed to bring me a dress from the laundry but she forgot so Mummy goes to find me one. Daddy brings a cake and candles. Mummy comes back with a pretty dress with tiny pink dots that stick out. It's a little small on me but I don't mind.

I light the candles with the good-luck candle. Everyone sings happy birthday. I blow out the candles and Mummy and Daddy lift my chair up six times. Mummy gives all the children a slice of cake and then they run to visit their parents.

We leave too. Mummy carries the rest of the cake to the Room so my brother David can have some too.

My birthday last year was in Camp Bilu'im. I don't remember a thing about it.

Celebration

Dori

Shoshana says she's going to read us a bedtime story if we're good. We brush our teeth and pee and get into our pyjamas. Shoshana sits on a chair between the bedrooms so everyone can hear. We can't see her but we hear her voice. I wonder why her voice is always hoarse. Most people only have a hoarse voice when they have a cold.

The story is about a girl who finds out that her Group is moving into a new Children's House. She likes the old Children's House so she gets some paint and paints it and then it looks like new and the children don't have to move. I don't know how anyone can write such a boring story.

The only good thing about the story is the girl's name—Rakefet.[41] That's my favourite flower and my favourite thing in the world. When I see one in a field I get full of happiness. Come to think of it, we haven't had a Hike in a while. Just to the chicken coop and back. No one even likes the chicken coop. It's very crowded and noisy and if you go inside with blood from a cut the chickens attack you and try to kill you.

After Shoshana leaves I feel like talking in English. Skye knows English from when she was in Boston. I say Skye do you want to talk in English? Skye says yes. I say how are you? She says fine how are you? I say I am not happy. Skye says why you are not happy? I say because the story was not good. Skye says yes it was not good. I'm getting tired of English. My brain isn't used to it any more. I say goodnight Skye and Skye says goodnight Dori.

The other children are jealous that we talked in English. I know it isn't nice. I want to be nice all the time but I can't.

Our First Year

8 March 1949. Our library is now open for business in its temporary quarters in a vaulted room in the two-storey building of Eldar's former mukhtar, or village chief. It's already one of the most popular spots in the kibbutz.

Dori

It's really quiet tonight. Really really quiet. I don't feel good. There's a song about this feeling—

92

In the dark a lone cat howls
Midnight trees softly shake
A fog drifts in from the sea
Only Anokhi is still awake

It's a lonely song with a lonely tune. In the black art book there's a man who reminds me of Anokhi.[42] He's walking in a swamp with a walking stick and holding his coat shut and there's a mysterious light behind him. When when when is Mummy or Daddy coming to kiss me goodnight?

Here she is here she is! I feel bad for the other children. They probably feel sick too but in their case they have to go on feeling sick until they fall asleep.

Mummy says *I'm so tired sweetie I'm falling asleep on my feet so just a quick kiss tonight.* She kisses me and says *Dori are you sure you still need these goodnight visits now that you're such a big girl?* I get very scared when she says that. I shout *yes yes I still need them* and she says *don't worry—no one is going to tell me what to do.* I knew she wouldn't stop. Not until I say.

I don't ask for a rhyme but she tells me one anyhow. She chooses the shortest rhyme she knows—

Up and down
Left and right
I like to fly my kite

It's a baby rhyme but who cares. At least she came. I feel better now.

Our First Year

13 March 1949. The bus made its first run to Haifa today! Historic local passengers were Isaac, Naftali, Amos and Dafna. It was the driver's first day on the line (Luigi is still in Haifa arranging for his busman's test) so naturally he spent most of the time watching the passing scenery rather than the road.

Today is Trumpeldor Day. There was a dramatization in the Dining Hall and then we marched to the top of Al-Tawil, the hill that lies to the west and from which one can see the lights both of Safed and Haifa. Full moon with a crisp wind a-blowing, so we could hardly wait to light our bonfire at the prescribed time, when fires were to blaze up in all the settlements of the countryside. Then a few selections from our pocket-sized choir, valiantly rendered, and a few words on the significance of the occasion by Martin.

When we got home we discovered that our tender—which is the name for any small pick-up truck in this country—had arrived from Galron, where it had been in repair for two months. Painted a brilliant green, and hunched up on its hind wheels and ready to roll. So our motor fleet has been doubled.

Dori

I'm on my way to Lulu's birthday party. Suddenly a boy from an older Group comes over and asks me if I want to see a shelter.

I say *yes*. I'm always interested in seeing new things.

He goes down a metal ladder. I go down after him but I stay on the ladder because I don't like it down here.

He says *do you want to do sex*?

I'm free but I don't like this boy. I run up the ladder and all the way to the Room. Now I'm crying. Daddy asks *what is it*? but I don't know why I'm crying.

Daddy says *I have a new book for you doda*. He shows me the book. It's called *Alice in Wonderland* and it's big and white like *Pinnochio*. I love the picture on the cover—a blonde girl in a red dress sitting in a field of flowers and looking at a rabbit. The rabbit is holding a clock and running.

I sit on Daddy's lap and he reads to me. This is the best book I've ever read in my entire life.

MARINA   My poor feet ... Thank God I'm not working tomorrow.

MICHAEL   Thank Eli, our lord and saviour.

ELI   *(smiling)* If you don't watch out, I'll put you in the kitchen for a year.

MARINA   Don't pay attention to him—he's mad because he can't drive his truck tomorrow. You know what? I don't care. Let him drive. Let him go back to his truck, his fun in the city, his Arab friends, his soldiers and girlfriends, I don't want him any more. I'm looking for a new husband. Put it on the agenda for this week's meeting: to be discussed, a replacement spouse for Marina.

RITA   You can have me, darling Marina. Any time. *(Raises volume of radio.)* May I have this dance? (RITA *and* MARINA *dance*)

MICHAEL   If you need me, I'll be praying. *(Exits)*

Dori

I really really don't want to go back tonight. I lie down on the sofa and pretend I'm asleep. That way Daddy will have to carry me. He lifts me on his back and I lean my head on his shoulder.

We walk to the Children's House. I keep my eyes closed and my arms around Daddy's neck.

I pretend to wake up when he says *we're here, doda.* I slide down from his back and he kisses me goodbye for now.

Lulu says *you didn't come to my birthday party—I'm five now.*

I completely forgot! I begin to cry. Lulu pats me on the back and says *never mind sweetie.* She says *there's cake left over and you'll come tomorrow and have a piece—hush now.*

Shoshana says *hurry up hurry hurry hurry.* Go to hell Shoshana. Go to hell and stay there.

I made a promise to myself in Canada about forgetting things. Mummy bought me a beautiful white sweater in a department store. It was so beautiful! With little pearls on the collar and shiny buttons. Mummy wasn't going to buy it because it cost a lot but when she saw how much I loved it she bought it. Then on the bus home we sat on a side seat and I put the sweater next to me and I told myself *don't forget the sweater!*

But then Mummy almost missed our stop and she was in a big rush and I forgot the sweater. She noticed as soon as we were out of the bus but it was too late. She started to be angry at me but then she decided it was her fault. I was sad and she was sadder.

I made a promise to myself never ever to forget anything again. But I still forget things. Not things that happen but things that don't happen. Like Lulu's party.

Our First Year

16 March 1949. Last night when the bus was returning from Nahariya it was stopped a few kilometres down the road. The driver claims that a large group of armed Arabs demanded that he take them to Lebanon. He refused, warning them that in the event of abduction a party would be sent out immediately and there would be the devil to pay.

For the next few days an armed guard will accompany him on his trip from Nahariya.

Dori

A woman with a camera comes to take photographs of us in the shower.[43] She talks with Shoshana and they both smile. Shoshana hides who she is with adults.

Everyone laughs and runs back and forth so the woman won't be able to take the photograph. As a matter of fact I want to be in the photograph. But I don't want anyone to know because no one else wants to be in it. I stand still and pretend to play with my fingers. It's fun to be in a photograph.

Another new thing today is a lesson on brushing our teeth. Shoshana says a dentist came to Eldar to give a lecture and he told everyone to brush up and down not across.

One of my teeth is loose as a matter of fact. I like moving it with my tongue. Jonathan says his father eats blood on bread. Disgusting!

Cropped by the Subject c. 1967

Dori

I had a dream that I was a baby lying in my crib. My Minder Doreet was looking down at me and smiling. Doreet has a big face and glasses and blonde hair that flies everywhere. She has a very nice smile and Mummy loves her. Mummy thinks I called my doll Doreet because I like Doreet but really it was because my doll had red hair which is close to blonde. People say I have red hair but I don't know why. It's blonde like Doreet's.

In the dream I looked up at Doreet from my crib and I was sure that my face looked like her face.

Now I'm awake but I still feel I have Doreet's face. Doreet isn't ugly but a little girl with a big loose face and big glasses is ugly. If I look in the mirror I can see that I don't look like Doreet but the minute I look away I see myself from the ceiling and what I see is Doreet.

I wonder what happened to that doll. I don't usually like dolls but in Canada I liked having something that was from Eldar. I gave us both a haircut and Mummy said *Dori what have you done!* She was a little angry but she also laughed though she tried not to.

Mummy said *now your doll won't have any hair.* I said *it'll grow back* and Mummy thought I really believed hair grows on dolls and she laughed very hard and told everyone. And now whenever she says *it'll grow back* everyone laughs.

I tried to explain but she didn't understand. Many things are hard to explain.

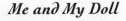

Me and My Doll

Dori

We're still reading *Alice in Wonderland*. Daddy asks if I want to play cards but all I want to do is read *Alice in Wonderland*. This is the best book anyone ever wrote. A hundred times better than *Pinocchio*.

I like the pictures too. The only one I don't like is when Alice only has a head and feet. That picture makes me feel a little sick. I try not to look at it.

When I grow up I want to write a book like *Alice in Wonderland*. I tell Daddy I'm going to be a writer. He laughs and says *that's wonderful dollie.*

Our First Year

17 March 1949. A quiet day in which a few of us with our mentor, Dov, took an inspection trip through our orchards. One of those unique tone poems of Eldar weather, a day to conjure with: flurries of rain and then sunshine, and sunshine through the rain with all those ancient and hackneyed but magnificent images of nature's spring beauty, huge drops of rain on broad green leaves, delicately coloured hyacinths, anemones, cyclamens appearing like flute obligatos from within the full orchestral rumble of rocks and weeds and trees, a straight and slimly formed apricot tree in glistening pinkish-orange blossom surrounded by gnarled olive trees, the terraces falling away like carpeted steps of deep green, diamond-sprinkled green, and swirls and patches of chartreuse, the deep, good, chocolate-brown earth in the valleys, so soft, so magnificently textured that one dreamily thinks of biting into a chunk ...

Dori

It's really hot today. Instead of staying in the Room we go out to the lawn and fill basins with water. In between sitting in the basin I stand on Daddy's shoulders and count. I can keep my balance to 100.

There are other adults on the lawn and everyone is talking and laughing. Daddy is explaining all sorts of things. He's very smart.

On the ship to Canada there was a pool. I was afraid to go inside it though. I didn't want to fall into the ocean.

I liked that ship. I didn't like the food but Daddy always tried to find something for me on the menu like bread or mashed potatoes.

A horrible thing happened on the ship. Right in the middle of supper two waiters dragged another waiter to the door and threw him out of the room and he fell on the floor. His body was all skinny and crooked and nervous and he was scared and trying to explain and stuttering but they wouldn't listen and didn't care.

I asked Daddy why they threw him out and Daddy didn't know what to say. Finally he said *because he spilled soup on someone* but he said it the way he says things he doesn't want to explain. How can you be angry with someone for spilling soup on a ship? The waves keep moving everything around.

I was sad and Daddy was sad too. I don't know why he didn't get up to help that man.

Steamship Zion

Dori

I'm remembering that ship. There was a girl on the ship who was my good friend. She didn't know any Hebrew or English but she knew what I meant and I knew what she meant. I wanted to be her friend forever but I don't even know where she is.

She looked like the girl in *Nariko-San, the Girl From Japan*. A blonde girl comes to visit Nariko-San in Japan and they change clothes. There are photographs of the whole visit.

I know that book by heart. I like it a lot more than *Dolly Ziva*. I like books that are real or not real. *Nariko-San, the Girl From Japan* is real and it has photographs. *Alice in Wonderland* isn't real. *Dolly Ziva* has photographs like *Nariko-San* but the story is about a doll that talks. Books like that don't make sense to me.

Genre Confusion

Dori

On my way to the Room I meet my brother David and Noam and Amnoni. They're going on an adventure. I ask if I can come but David says *oh no there will be huge huge rivers that you have to cross* and Noam says *and huge thorns* and Amnoni says *and gigantic scorpions that if they bite you you die right away.*

I don't know if they're telling the truth. They're not allowed to lie so I have to believe them but I think they might be lying. I really want to go with them but there's nothing I can say.

I get to the Room in a bad mood. I tell Daddy *David and Noam and Amnoni won't let me go with them on their adventure*. Daddy laughs. I don't know what's so funny.

I tell Daddy we're going to start school soon. Not here—in Galron. That's the closest kibbutz. We'll be getting there on a microbus.

I wasn't there when Shoshana told everyone. I was outside on the monkey bars. When I came in everyone was shouting *we're going on a microbus we're going on a microbus!*

They were very excited so I tried to be excited. But the truth is I don't know what a microbus is.

Our First Year

1 April 1949. Friday night celebration in which the priest from Jish delivered a lecture, in Hebrew, on the historical background of the area. An impressive-looking man, short, stout, barbed, clad in a long black cassock, and wearing a large pith helmet—Livingstone out of darkest Africa.

Some of us had a good deal of trouble understanding the Hebrew.

Dori

Mummy has a new thing she says—

> *Shut up fool*
> *You're talking tosh*
> *You have the brain*
> *Of half a squash*

She says it over and over. It makes her laugh very hard.

I don't know why it makes her laugh. Daddy told me never to say *shut up* to anyone.

But I don't care. When Mummy's happy I'm happy.

Transcript of Meeting
April 1961

Topic: Hired labour
Chair: Isaac Milman

Isaac: Tamir and Emanuel claim that "We need hired labour or we can't manage; we can't run the kibbutz properly without it; produce will die; it makes no economic sense; we don't have the manpower and we don't have the volunteers; we will never be able to sustain this enterprise if we don't hire Arab locals, for whom it would be a real boost."

Oded: Tamir and Emanuel are a hundred percent right and this is an urgent matter. As Economic Coordinator, I can't stress this enough.

Naftali: Please remember that Economic Coordinator is not a position of authority, and you don't have any special powers vested in you.

Oded: I resent your tone and your implications.

Isaac: Fellows, fellows, let's keep this on an appropriate level, please.

Martin: As you know, I'm probably the person who has the most contact, along with Isaac, with our neighbours.

Isaac: You can have that position for yourself, seeing as you're the only one who's mastered Arabic ...

Martin: I know that we have well-founded reasons for rejecting a structure we came here to escape. Nevertheless we believe in helping our brothers and I know how welcome jobs would be. An employer need not be an exploiter, necessarily. I think that with all due respect, this would help our neighbours feed their families with income from picking. And, by the way, the offer from Jish to set up another course in Arabic is ongoing.

Varda: Why am I having déjà vu? Didn't we discuss all this last year, and the year before, and the year before?

Yael:	That's exactly the point. We need a policy for the sake of efficiency and so we can plan ahead.
Lou:	A kibbutz that depends on outsiders as a matter of course is not a kibbutz.
Martin:	Let's invite them all to join …

Dori

My brother David says that today is a holiday for religious people where they don't eat all day. He says we're having extra food to show we don't care.

Noam says magicians know how to make people disappear. I tell him it isn't true but Amnoni and David say it is. They say a person can disappear forever if the magician forgets the right words to bring them back.

I know it isn't true but I ask Daddy anyhow. He says magicians use tricks and really the person is hiding in a box or under the table.

In a scary movie I saw on television in Canada a man got trapped in a wall. Right inside it. I don't remember how he got there in the first place but he couldn't get out. No one could hear him calling for help.

I ask Daddy if I can have extra soup almonds because of the holiday. He doesn't know what I'm talking about. They made that holiday up too.

Thane of Elðar

I escaped the hunt. Yet this too is heavy sentence, my native English now I must forgo, within my mouth you have enjailed my tongue. Oh dateless limit of my exile, the hopeless word of never to return. Blow, wind! Come, wrack! At least we'll die with harness on our back!

Dori

It's naptime but I'm not tired. I get up and look around for anyone who's awake. I know I'll be in trouble if Shoshana comes back but she doesn't usually come during the nap.

Everyone in my room is asleep. I go to the other room and see that Gilead is awake. He's bored too but he has a better idea than just talking. He whispers *do you want to run away*? I nod and we sneak out of the Children's House. It's a lucky thing I finally learned how to tie my shoelaces.

We don't want anyone to see us so we run in a direction that isn't the Rooms or the fields or the barns. We have to sneak past the cabin where Mummy teaches. We're having a real adventure.

We see a man sitting on a rock and peeling a stick with a knife. He has a little fire with potatoes inside. I don't know if he's from Eldar. I don't think so because you're not supposed to have your own food on Eldar.

We say hello and he says hello back. Gilead asks *how come your teeth are yellow*? The man says *because I don't brush them*. Gilead asks *how come you don't brush them*? but he doesn't answer.

It's very hot and we start getting thirsty. We decide to go back to the Children's House for the Wake-Up snack. We're a bit scared now.

Fortunately Simon's mother is doing the Wake-Up today. She doesn't care that we ran away. Everyone says *we're going to tell Shoshana*. I'm a little worried about that.

Our First Year

8 April 1949. A movie this evening, but without sound. We got the idea that Rita Hayworth was a very naughty girl and that somebody was trying to kill somebody. A number of people became quite enthusiastic and elaborate in ad libbing the sound track. Unfortunately we don't seem to have much control over the films we will be receiving in the future (our machine will arrive shortly), and we anticipate cinematographic torture.

Dori

We're being wild during naptime. We're getting out of our beds and running around and laughing. Lulu comes to visit from the other bedroom.

We thought Shoshana was gone but here she is. She goes from bed to bed and hits us one by one.

But I trick her. I pretend to cry before it hurts. As soon as I cry she stops and moves on to Elan.

The only person she doesn't hit is Skye. That's because Skye didn't leave her bed. That way as soon as Shoshana came in she could pretend she was asleep. I told you Skye was smart.

Shoshana never hit me before. She's afraid of Daddy. I'm surprised she took a chance this time.[44]

Baby Diary

July 13
I'm very depressed because of her rash. It's on her face, ears, head, forehead, it's horrible. I decided she wouldn't get a bottle with cow's milk for her sixth feeding if she wakes up. Maybe the milk is causing the rash.

Dori

On the way to the Room I see a new girl near the swings. She's smaller than me and her face and neck are covered with scars. I'm not sure if she's coming to live here or just visiting. Someone said her scars are from boiling water but someone else said she was born with them.

I want to be nice to her so I tell her she can sit on the swing and I'll push. I think she's only visiting because she's wearing a pleated skirt with red and black squares. Eldar doesn't have those kind of skirts.

She sits on the swing and I push her but then my shoe-lace gets undone so I say *just a second* and I bend down to tie it. She lifts the swing and pushes it as hard as she can. The swing hits me right on my forehead and I fall backwards. The little girl runs away. Hard to believe but she did it on purpose.

I have tears in my eyes because of how much my forehead hurts but I decide not to cry. I could cry but I'm not going to.

Transcript of Meeting
May 1961

Topic:	Status of Naftali
Chair:	Isaac Milman

Isaac: I want to make it clear first of all that I was pressured into putting this on the agenda by a relentless campaign on the part of several of our younger members,[45] but I do not support the topic—I reject it entirely. I feel it's harassment, and I'm informing everyone in advance that if the vote goes against Naftali I'm resigning from the Secretariat and possibly taking more drastic steps. A group of seven members—Tamir, Oded, Nurit, Yael, Emanuel, Katzi and Ora—claim that "Naftali had a four-month leave and stayed in Canada nearly two years and therefore should be demoted to candidacy status."

Varda: [Bursts into tears.]

Naftali: I have nothing to contribute to this discussion. Neither does Varda. Come on, Varda, let's go.
[They leave.]

Yael: I'm sorry, but everyone is expected to follow the rules that we all agreed on as a group. Naftali broke the rules unilaterally.

Tamir: If he's allowed to come and go as he pleases, then the voting procedure is meaningless.

Oded: It's not as if there was even a reason. He wanted to write a novel. That is entirely against everything we believe in.

Martin: When exactly did we stop believing in art? I think I missed that day.

Isaac: We do in fact have a policy that artists get extra time to work on their art.

Oded: Yes, but not a whole year. Besides, you have to prove yourself first, publish at least a story or a few poems. Anyone can call himself a writer. Has anyone read his book?

Coco: The fact is, it was published.

Oded: I've heard he paid to have it published.

Isaac: We're getting off-topic. The literary merit of Naftali's book is not the issue.

Nurit: I agree. The issue is that he stayed away and the reason is irrelevant. Even if his parents were dying, let's say, it wouldn't be relevant. The point is that an extension was not approved.

Isaac: It may be difficult for the younger members to grasp what Naftali contributed from day one, what sort of conditions we endured. Ten years of devoted hard labour, day in day out, count for something.

Martin: "Saint Peter don't you call me, cause I can't go ..."

Isaac: I suggest we set up a special committee to see what other Shomer kibbutzim have done in similar cases and proceed from there. All in favour?

Dori

In Canada I had two dresses I loved. Pioneers aren't supposed to like dresses but I couldn't help it. One was a red velvet jumper with a white lace blouse. The red was the most beautiful red in the world and the blouse had a lace collar and pearl buttons. When I wore it I felt like a piece of cake with icing.

The second dress had black and white stripes and buttons like jewels. I wanted to keep it for the rest of my life but I don't know where it is now.

I wish I still had it. I wish I wish I wish.

Our First Year

3 May 1949. A number of our comrades accepted an invitation to see a play staged by the schoolchildren of Jish. Another enjoyable experience in cementing Jewish–Arab friendship.

Dori

It's Sukkot today. What a *balagan!*[46] We're supposed to decorate a sukkah but we don't know which one or where. We go to the older Group's sukkah but they don't want us there. We go to the younger Group's sukkah but it's already decorated. We run back and forth back and forth all day long looking for a sukkah to decorate.

In the end I go to the Room and Daddy gives me some figs but they're the dried kind. I haven't had a fig from a tree in a long time. They're hard to find.

Mummy comes into the Room. She looks very tired. She sits down on the sofa and we read from the English rhyme book. She loves that book.[47] The drawings only have three colours—red and blue and yellow—but most of them are pretty. Mummy likes rhymes I don't really understand—

The king of France
With forty thousand men
Rode up the hill
And then came down again

or

Hickory dickory dock
The mouse ran up the clock
The clock struck one
The mouse ran down
Hickory dickory dock

There isn't much of a story there. There's a beginning and an end but nothing in the middle. But they make Mummy laugh.

Then we sing Au clair de la Lune—

Au clair de la lune
Mon ami Pierrot
Prtmoitplmprecrirunmo
Ma chandelle est morte
Jnpltfeu
Ovrmtprt
Pour l'amour de dieu

Now that is a good story.

Thy Neck with Chains of Gold

RITA   I once told you I don't want anyone watching over me. You act as if you have special privileges.

RICKY   I thought I *did* have special privileges. Maybe it's my imagination, but didn't we at one time take long walks in the field and talk about our dreams? Before you started going into town to visit your *cousin*.

RITA   Look, Ricky. I want my own room, I want to do what I want when I want. I don't want to be tied down.

RICKY   Don't give me that claptrap. I know you better than anyone around here. You always asked me to be with you
when you were alone, to listen to your thoughts, sympa-
thize with your aches and pains. I read Omar Khayyam
to you to help you fall asleep. And when you quarrelled
with one of the girls, on whose shoulder did you cry?

RITA   Ricky, maybe you should find—

RICKY   Let's get married. How about tomorrow?

Dori

Jonathan's leaving Eldar! He's going to another kibbutz with his parents.

I think it's because of his father. His father who eats blood. Because when I told Daddy about the blood he didn't want to talk about it but he believed me and he said *nothing about Oded would surprise me.*

Jonathan's leaving tomorrow morning. This is our last time in the same Group.

Baby Diary

July 14

The doctor saw the rash, suggested putting [illegible] for a few days. He said it's not serious, rather something that is common to many babies. She's very cute. She's quiet, easy, sleeps well, and is growing. She already doesn't look like a new baby. Her face is pretty, sweet. The order of her feedings today was: I gave all the feedings 4:00 a.m.–8:00–11:00–3:30–6:30–midnight–6:30. [sic]

Today Naftali took David to Nahariya. I don't feel pressured to spend time with him. It's completely different with two children. Even though I feel more confident and calm with Dori compared to my experience with a first child, I want to spend time with David. I also worry about him but I can't devote myself to him as before. Sometimes it works out that I can be with him the entire evening and sometimes almost nothing at all.

And also all Dori's accomplishments, I don't manage to switch with Naftali at the moment that she does them. With David we were always together in the evening. Now I'm completely alone. Naftali visits during the day but it's not the same.

Dori

That whole business with tying Elan to the bed again. I'm really getting fed up with that business.

At least this time we didn't have to watch.

Our First Year

4 May 1949. Most of the ploughing for the vegetable gardens has been completed.

The 60 dunams or so of Arab grapevines have been pruned.

One of the buildings has been converted into a chicken run.

A new machine and tool shed is under construction.

Sturdily and attractively designed new tables have been finished by our carpentry shop for the new Dining Hall, which will soon be ready for use.

Our first fifty pullets arrived, and we are anxiously awaiting the arrival of a thousand chicks.

Dori

That Alice in Wonderland.

If you're going to turn into a pig dear I'll have nothing more to do with you. I laugh and Daddy laughs and we both laugh until we can't stop.

Daddy puts on the radio to hear the news. I don't understand a single word. It's in Hebrew but not the kind I know.

The man on the radio says *good evening* and Daddy answers *good evening*. I ask Daddy *why do you say good evening—you know he can't hear you*. Daddy smiles and says *it's friendly*.

I make a fist and bang the bump on Daddy's forehead because that doesn't exactly make sense. I ask *why is Jonathan leaving?* but Daddy doesn't want to say. I ask *can we go visit him on his new kibbutz* and he says *it might be hard to get there*. I ask *is it far* and he doesn't know what to say. Finally he says *it might be complicated to get there*. I guess it's far away across the mountains.

The *pundak*[48] song comes on. I love that song. It's my favourite song in Hebrew—

> *And the balladeer said*
> *Never mind never mind*
> *And he raised a glass*
> *To the heroes of the past*
> *In the smoke*—whistle, cluck—*of the small*
> *pundak*

I don't know all the words and I don't know what a *pundak* is or a balladeer but I love the tune and how the balladeer says *never mind never mind* and the whistle and cluck. I asked Daddy what a *pundak* is but he shrugged his shoulders and didn't know what to say. Finally he said *a place where people sit*. Why would there be a word for a place where people sit?

I actually had a record in Canada with the *pundak* song but unfortunately I sat on it by mistake and it broke into two pieces. I cried and cried but Daddy laughed. He said he'd get another one but he couldn't find that record in Canada.

Eldar Eldar Eldar.

Elðar Elðar Elðar

Dori

I really really don't want to go back tonight. I'm going to say I'm sick and then Daddy will have to stay with me.

I say *I think I have fever.* Daddy kisses my forehead and says *when we get to the Children's House we'll take your temperature.*

He asks if I want him to carry me and I climb on his back. If only the Children's House was a thousand kilometres away.

Before you know it we're here. Daddy lets me down and tells Shoshana *I promised Dori we'd take her temperature.* Shoshana brings the thermometer to the entrance. Daddy never comes in more than the entrance unless it's for my goodnight kiss. Shoshana hands me the thermometer but somehow it slips and falls on the floor and breaks into tiny pieces. Shoshana and Daddy burst out laughing.

Everyone has to stay away while Shoshana picks up the pieces with a dustpan because if mercury gets into your body you die.

Daddy and Shoshana laugh some more and then he leaves. I don't understand this at all. How come if the thermometer broke it means I'm not sick? And how come if a thermometer breaks it's funny?

I begin to cry. I sit on my chair and cry right through supper. There's tongue for supper. A cow's tongue. Disgusting if you ask me but I'm hungry so I eat it. I eat it and cry and Shoshana laughs at me because I have to stop crying every time I take a bite.

Baby Diary

November 22

I handed over the 2:00 feeding to the Minder, Edna. How strange it was not to come to her again at that hour! I felt something was missing. But it seems I didn't regret it as much as I did when I handed over the feeding with David. My work keeps me so busy and so utterly depleted of energy, that the extra rest is quite simply healing. But that's not to say that I don't feel a sense of longing. I hurry to her earlier than the other mothers, to kiss her delicious soft cheeks, to hug her close to me.

She turns in a circle on her belly. Today she did a full circle. She also raises her legs forward, a hint of the crawling that will soon come. She's patient, kind-hearted, and always happy.

She won't receive a full bottle but rather pudding in a cup. She doesn't suck much at that hour anyhow.

Dori

Usually Shoshana wakes us in the morning but today we woke up by ourselves. There's no one here—only us.

We go wild. Lulu and Gilead come into our room and we all get wild together. We scream and yell and jump on the beds. We spill the peepee from the potty on Elan's bed.

Elan gets very scared. He stands on his bed with his back against the wall and his hands against the wall and he shivers and smiles in that worried way. I feel bad for him but I try not to think about it. He makes tiny scared sounds while he shivers. We push him down on the bed. He tries to get up and we push him down again.

Only Skye doesn't join us. She stays in her bed and watches.

Our First Year

18 May 1949. Worked in our vineyards today, elevating the vines on crossed stakes. Long, black, gnarled vines, twisting along the ground, with the green new growths being stuck up into the air like giant fans.

Beautiful day; every morning the long walk down the slope, a gothic descent from our castle-like home along stony paths strung with thorns, slabs and tables of rocks, with ants, chameleons, and busy insects covering the earth with a lacework of agitated life and movement.

The view from the south hill towards the village is toy-like, magical. Fig trees like flat candy dishes on a white stem of glass, the olive trees like balls of rich, deep silver-green, the terraces like pebble fences, the fields of poppies and the blue stuff like a wash of water colour, the aluminum roofs on the wood huts gleam with an intensity that makes them more fierce-looking than the sun, the brown ploughed patches, the fields of grass, the parched boulders and out-croppings—can anything in the country compare with our Eldar?

Dori

Everything is taking me a long time today. The other children already left to visit their parents but I'm still eating my bread and jam.

It's quiet in the Children's House with no one here. I get that feeling again—the feeling that I have Doreet's big loose face. I'm very ugly with that face.

My hands are full of sticky jam so I go to the sink to wash them. I'm wondering—do your hands get cleaner the more times you wash them? I wash my hands over and over and then I run very fast to the Room without touching anything and I say to Daddy *do my hands look clean*? And he says *yes very clean* and I say *really really really clean*? And he says *yes really really clean* but I can tell he's only trying to make me happy.

That was an experiment. I proved that if you wash your hands one time or a lot of times it's exactly the same. Exactly exactly the same.

Precedents

Out, out damn spot!

Dori

It's our day to go to Galron. Everyone's shouting *microbus microbus*! But you know what? In the end a microbus is just a small bus.

I sit next to Skye. Suddenly I remember about the shelter. I ask Skye *do you know what a shelter is*? Skye says *they're in case the Enemy drops a bomb on us.*

I say *a boy asked me to do sex in there.* Skye says *he asked Hagar too but it hurt so she told him to stop. I heard her tell my sister.* I say *I didn't like him.* Skye says *he's new here.*

Skye reads the sign on the road. She knows how to read because her father taught her. I think I know who her father is. I think he's the serious man with the moustache. Serious like Skye.

Transcript of Meeting
August 1961

Topic: Integration of Outside Students—Parental Votes
Chair: Amos Atar

Amos: It was suggested at the last meeting that the parents of each high-school grade be allowed to decide by majority vote on integration for that grade.

This is our umpteenth meeting on this topic and I'd like to make a request that points which have already been made should not be made again. We're here to vote on a specific topic which came up at the last meeting but which we didn't have time to discuss.

To summarize the points which have already been made, I have made a list, which I'd like to present, in no particular order:

a) segregation reminds us of Jim Crow;

b) we need members and these children are more likely to stay if we integrate them completely;

c) if we don't take in outside children, our own children won't be able to be educated here as we don't have the numbers to create a high-school facility, and that means we'll only see them on the weekend;

d) children who may be disturbed, wild, or even delinquent will have a bad effect on our own children and may bring discord into their lives;

e) this has nothing to do with Jim Crow because these children are not average children and our doubts have nothing whatsoever to do with race or city background (on the contrary, we want as mixed a population as possible) but with the fact that many of the children are troubled due to early experiences;

f) we are teaching our children to accept and educate others and to be inclusive—what better opportunity is there to put those values into daily practice;

g) we believe the influence will work in the other direction, and this belief in education is at the heart of all we hold dear;

h) it is our moral duty to help others in need, and to quote the Talmud, "if I am only for myself, what am I?" not to mention Marx et. al.;

i) these are Israeli children and their conditions have been deplorable, the country must do all that it can to help them, and we are duty-bound to try and remedy the neglect they have suffered;

j) we don't have the resources to accept high-school children and segregate them so it's either integrate them or not take them at all;

k) we are doing more than our share already—we've taken in many social service cases largely at our own expense;

l) can we afford a high-school in the first place?

m) we have successfully integrated the young outside children sent to us by social services;

n) not everyone agrees that this has been an unqualified success.

Have I covered everything?

Varda: Thank you, Amos, that's very helpful.

Naftali: Yes, very well done.

Amos: What we're voting on today is the proposal that came up last week. The proposal is that we allow the parents of each grade to vote on whether they agree to integration for their children. And now I would be most grateful if someone else took over as I'm running a fever and should really be in bed.

Dori

We're here!

The Galron Group is much bigger than ours. Their teacher is called Carmella and her hair is really the colour of caramel. What surprises me is that her hair is puffed! I guess they don't care as much about things like that in Galron. Or else they care but Carmella doesn't care.

Mummy says hair that's all done up makes women look like they have a cake on their head. It makes Mummy laugh to say *a cake on their head* and I laugh with her. But Carmella doesn't have a cake on her head. She only has a bit of a puff.

Carmella has a nice smile. She's a sleepy person. She likes to sit on a chair and when she needs something she asks a child to get it for her. She asks very nicely with her nice smile. I like her.

We play with new toys. I find a hammering toy. We used to have a hammering toy in Eldar but I haven't seen it in a while. I like that toy. You hammer the pieces of wood down through the holes then you turn it around and hammer them the other way. It sounds boring but it's fun. Fun to see the pieces go down until they're flat. Boom boom boom.

Carmella writes a sentence on the board and tells us we can copy what she wrote on a piece of paper and draw a picture underneath. We all sit at tables and copy the words and draw pictures. Then we go out to the playground to play. Then we have juice and crackers and then the microbus comes to take us home.

I like school.

22 September 1955

Two Killed and Ten Wounded in Infiltrator Attack

Infiltrators yesterday shot at a bus heading towards Meron. Our correspondent in Safed reports that at 7:30 PM the Haifa-Safed bus was attacked on the incline between Kibbutz Eldar and Meron, about 150 metres from the moshav. Gunfire opened from two positions and two hand grenades were thrown.

The wounded driver maintained control of the vehicle until the last minute and was able to prevent it from rolling into the wadi. He had time to call out, 'I have a gun, take it,' before collapsing. The shooting continued for three to four minutes. A truck driver stopped to assist the passengers. Armed Meron residents rushed to the scene and helped the wounded. One of the dead was a tourist from the United States.

The Northern Police Force immediately brought in hundreds of police officers to search the area. It is believed that the infiltrators came from Lebanon. Local scouts and search dogs were used in the search and escape routes were blocked. The Israeli delegation to the Israel-Lebanon Armistice Commission informed the Observers of the event and will submit a strongly worded complaint to the Chairman of the Commission.

—*Davar*, 23 September, 1955

Meron Killers Came from Lebanon, Had Local Assistance

Four local trackers, accompanied by U.N. Observers, crossed the border into Lebanon in pursuit of the killers who attacked the bus near Meron. According to the latest information, the Thursday attack was carried out by four men. A large-scale search led to the discovery of two warehouses in the vicinity, one containing Sten guns and the other Bern rifles and hundreds of bullets. The bullets match those removed from the victims. According to reliable sources, there is no truth to the rumour that the infiltrators scattered landmines as they retreated. The police extended their search to minority villages and arrested four men from Rehaniya.

An American tourist was killed in the attack. David Barak, whose father was killed by the Nazis, was engaged to a resident of Jaffa. He was planning to marry his fiancée after the Day of

Atonement and settle in Israel. He exchanged words of Torah with a fellow passenger during the entire trip. When the shots rang out at 7:05, the driver turned off the lights and struggled to bring the vehicle to a halt even though he was bleeding. One of the passengers, Yakov Gisheid, from Sfat Emet Yeshiva in Jerusalem, called for everyone to lie on the floor. Shortly afterwards, truck driver Dov Horan entered the bus and, with the help of Mr. Gisheid, carried everyone out of the bus. Two more cars passed; the first quickly left the scene while the other, a military vehicle, stopped and helped transport the wounded.

The second fatality, Malka Granot, 29, of Eldar, was laid to rest today in the Mount Eldar cemetery. Malka Granot boarded the bus at Kibbutz Eldar and sat near the driver. She was born in Paris, came to Israel at age three and studied in Jerusalem to be a teacher. She leaves behind Danny, five, and Ruti, two and a half. Her husband Eliezer, a member of Eldar, is a writer with a forthcoming book of poems. Malka Granot fought in the battle for Jerusalem during the War of Independence.

—*Davar*, 25 September 1955

Dori

I ask Skye whether the earth is spinning so fast we can't feel it or so slow we can't feel it. My brother David said fast but someone else said slow. I asked Daddy but I didn't understand his answer. He doesn't like questions about the planet.

Skye says *the earth is spinning very fast which gives us day and night and it moves even faster around the sun which gives us a year.* She says *you can't feel it moving because everything else is moving too and the reason you don't fall into space is gravity.*

I already know about gravity—though I don't understand why an apple gave Newton the idea. He saw things fall all the time.

William Tell is another person I don't understand. Why would anyone take a chance like that?

III

The Last Rain

I will give you the rain of your land in its season, the First Rain and the Last Rain, that you may gather in your grain, your sweet wine, your pure oil.

—DEUTERONOMY 11:14

Dori

Oh no! Not another thorn! I don't know how I get these thorns. I had a thorn in Camp Bilu'im and Daddy had to burn a needle to kill the germs. Then he used the needle to take it out and it hurt. We still have that black needle.

I tell Daddy I have a thorn but I don't want him to take it out. He says he has to bring clothes to the laundry so we'll do that first.

It's fun in the laundry. There are holes in the floor and Daddy tells me what to throw in each one. The clothes get washed and ironed under the floor. Simon's mother works down there. She comes up to say hello.

When we're finished Daddy looks at the thorn and says it's only half under the skin so maybe Dafna can pull it out and then it won't hurt. The whole way to Dafna I'm hoping.

We get to the infirmary and Dafna says she thinks she can pull it out with tweezers. Tweezers. A very good thing those tweezers. Dafna pulls and out it comes!

I'm a very lucky girl today.

Our First Year

27 May 1949. For a number of weeks a crew has been working on the pipeline of three and a half kilometers which will bring us water from the wadi that lies to the south-west of the village. It won't be a great deal, just enough to take care of our cooking and washing needs. Today the last section of the pipe was placed, and in the evening there was a party and a good old slapstick skit commemorating certain construction incidents.

The water problem still looms as one of our chief worries. We expect the experts, including Professor Picard, to make investigations in the area shortly.

Dori

Carmella tells us we're going on a Hike. We all get happy. Shoshana takes us on Hikes but they're very short. We visit the cows and the carpentry shop and then we go back. We hardly see nature at all.

This Hike is nice and long. It's on a road with fields full of wildflowers and wheat-stalks. I love the wheat-stalks. I love to pull them out and feel them on my face. There's the kind that feel like straw and the kind you can hold at the bottom and push up and all the pieces come off together.

This is the best Hike of my life. Everything is beautiful. There's a whole field of red anemones! Shiny red with black in the middle. Maybe if we're lucky we'll even see a cyclamen under a rock.

We stop at a waterfall. Carmella sits on a rock and shows us how to make cups out of paper and we all drink water. Running water is safe to drink.

Carmella says she's too tired to get up. She asks one of us to fill her cup and bring her water. I really like this Carmella.

Minders

In one study, only one of twenty Minders rated at the "excellent" level in a competency test based on the YG Federation's educational standards, including patience, understanding and commitment. Six rated very low, and one was seen to be a "tragic error."[49]

Dori

My brother David tells me there's going to be a movie near the carpentry shop. I'm on my way to the Room but I go with him instead. It's Saturday so I don't have to worry. On Saturdays we have the whole afternoon and evening to visit our parents.

Maybe the movie will be *Popeye*. I love Popeye. I love his funny voice and how he always saves Olivoil. *I'm Popeye the sailor man I'm Popeye the sailor man—ta dum ta da dum ta da dum ta da dum—I'm Popeye the sailor man.*

I help with putting the chairs in rows. Then we have to wait for the projector. It's a long wait.

Then the projector arrives but it's not working and someone has to come and fix it. I've never been so bored in my life. David is talking to his friends. Lulu shows up but then she leaves. She doesn't want to wait.

Finally the movie starts. It's called *For Him the Bell Tells*. I sit next to David so he can explain it to me. First a train explodes then a lot of Enemy soldiers chase two men with their rifles. Then one of the men gets shot and his friend has to kill him because he's going to die anyway. Then there's another explosion and parts of the ceiling fall down. After that there's a very long conversation. Very long. All David says is *now they're talking* which I can see for myself.

I leave and run to the Room. When I get there Daddy says it's time to go back.

That's it. I've had it. I'm completely fed up. I have a big tantrum.

A tantrum means you lie down in the doorway on your back and cry as loud as you can. The rule in Eldar is to ignore a child who has a tantrum. Just wait until the child gets tired.

That's fine with me. The longer I can keep up my tantrum the longer I get to stay in the Room. So I'll miss supper. So what.

Drinking and Crying

Dori

In Galron we get to make buns on Fridays. You braid
the dough and put on egg yolk with your fingers and
poppy seeds and Carmella bakes it in the oven. Then out
it comes—a delicious bun. You can eat it or take it as a
present to your parents.

That's hard to decide. Very hard. I eat half and save the
other half for Daddy. But he only takes a very small bite.
He says it's delicious and tells me to eat the rest.

I'm not as nice as Lulu. She shares her little round
box of candies with me even though they're just for her.
I'm not sure where her parents find the candies or how
they're allowed to give their child candies that are just for
her. My favourites are the pink ones with almonds inside.

The truth is that if my parents gave me a treat I
wouldn't share it with Lulu. I wouldn't share it with anyone. That's the truth.

Our First Year

3 June 1949. The garage is finished—a construction of aluminum sheeting on I-beams salvaged from the village. It's located in one of our oldest olive groves, some of whose trees we're told were planted in the days of Caesar. Imagine one of the old boy's phalanxes in our garage ...

Dori

School is a lot of fun. We go on long Hikes or we play in the yard or we play indoors. We copy words. Then we go back to playing. I can write my name now but I can't read it.

Everyone says that Gilead pulled out a child's fillings playing dentist but I don't know if it's true. I'm not sure a child can pull out a filling.

My brother David and Noam and Amnoni have been singing a mischievous song lately—

> *Yes we are cavaliers*
> *Though we have no horses*
> *If you ask on what we ride*
> *We ride on our lasses*

The song makes them laugh but I don't understand why. Why is it mischievous to ride on lasses? Maybe it means sex but how is sex mischievous and how is riding like sex? You do sex standing up.

Diary of a Young Man[50]

29 January 1922. Since we've established our commune, new people have come to join us daily. They're all "Shomrim" [members of Young Guard] from every corner of the world; some were part of the Tiberius road "work brigade," some came from the Hartiya road, others from the Afula-Nazareth road.

Our camp, white and sparkling, stands proudly on the slopes of the Carmel. We are three to four per tent; a few boards around a central pole serve as our table, and the beds are our chairs; in the young women's tent there's a white tablecloth, a vase of flowers, glowing pictures and a polished lamp.

Our only work is paving the road from the new [Jewish] neighbourhood [Neve Sha'anan on Mount Carmel] to the city [the lower part of Haifa]. The work is arduous, but most of us are veteran road workers and we're used to it.

Dori

Some children have teeny-tiny dolls. As small as my fingernail. I don't know where they come from. I really want a doll like that so I asked Daddy next time he goes to the city to buy me one.

He bought me a doll but it's way too big! It's the size of my finger not my fingernail. I cry and say *no no I wanted a teeny-tiny doll!* He laughs and says *I couldn't find a smaller one.*

I feel bad when he says that. He looked and looked but he couldn't find. And now I'm complaining instead of being happy.

He says he'll make me a chair and a bed for the doll. We go to the garage and get metal. Daddy cuts the metal with special scissors and bends it with pliers and makes little chairs and tables and beds. We put the doll furniture on a wooden tray. I'm happy for real now. The dolls are a little too big but they have wonderful furniture. And Daddy made it.

Our First Year

22 June 1949. Two of us got up at 4:30 this morning to dust the vines.

An early rising in the kibbutz is always tough but also refreshing: deserted grounds and a brilliant sunrise, the clean empty kitchen into which one stumbles rubbing one's eyes, the Primus humming away and the sleepy-eyed cook and first helper moving heavily about; something different, usually a bit better to eat; and that rare atmosphere of intimacy and unanimity, of calmness and order, before the hectic day explodes.

We used portable back and stomach dusters. The stuff puffs its way out in a foggy little cloud and settles on the leaves like powdered sugar being lightly sprinkled on doughnuts.

Amazing to think that this yellowish powder—consisting of sulphur, lime, and sodium fluo-something-or-other—is going to keep these beautiful, green, carved platters of leaves from being attacked by various insidious insects and diseases.[51]

Dori

Lulu has chicken pox. Shoshana tapes sticking plaster with our name on it to the back of our plates and tells us not to touch Lulu. But Daddy says you can't have chicken pox twice and it's better to have it when you're little.

If I get chicken pox Mummy and Daddy will be able to visit me right in the middle of the day. So when I play cards with Lulu on her bed and no one's looking I touch her pyjamas.

I hope it works.

Baby Diary

November 23
Didn't eat anything from Edna at 2:00. Only ate a drop of pudding and refused the rest. Simply shut her mouth ...

Very sociable. Laughs at everyone—also at the children next to her, Simon, Niv.

Dori

I have chicken pox. Everyone has it except for Skye because she had it in Boston. This morning she had to go to Galron all by herself.

Now she's back. She's showing off the puppet she made there. The puppet has a red satin gown that covers your hand when you hold it. She says *we had so much fun today so much fun* over and over and over. We all feel bad that we missed making puppets but we pretend not to care.

I don't like having chicken pox. I feel sick and thirsty all the time and my spots are itchy. But at least Mummy and Daddy were in and out all day long.

Diary of a Young Man

5 February 1922. Yesterday at the Meeting we had a lengthy discussion about our attitude to work. There are those who claim that we, the Shomrim, must be extra punctilious, because there are still stories circulating about Shomrim who go out to work and, when they should be paying attention to their tools, Nietzsche and Freud pour forth instead from their bosom.

Others feel that it doesn't matter what people say; we must direct our efforts first and foremost to creating a new society and living our collective lives in the most profound way possible.

Dori

We all have worms. Everyone except Skye.

The way to get rid of worms is an enema. Daddy takes me to the infirmary and fills my tushi with soapy water. I run to the toilet and out comes all the water. With the worms I hope.

My brother David has another method. You put lots of soap and water on a piece of toilet paper and then you stick it in your tushi. I'll try that next time.

Skye's grandmother in Boston sent her a necklace with a gold heart. The only thing we're allowed to have that's our own in the Children's House is our toothbrush because of germs and our shoes and slippers because someone else's wouldn't fit. But that bracelet could fit anyone.

But it's only Skye's.

Transcript of the Social Committee Meeting December 1961

Chair: Gila
Present: Martin, Shula, Lou, Varda, Hanan, Ora

Gila: The question we have to decide on is whether or not to suggest a reassessment of our personal property policy at the Meeting, and if so, what sort of changes we propose. There have been a lot of hard feelings lately about gifts individual members are getting, especially the Israeli members, who bring things back with them almost every weekend.

Ora: I don't know why you're always picking on the sabras. You guys get plenty of gifts from home.

Lou: Either way, as the standard of living rises, maybe we can afford to be more flexible.

Varda: True. Remember the fuss about the two kerosene lamps that you-know-who found in one of the Arab houses! Two lousy kerosene lamps, I think we discussed it until 2 a.m.

Martin: Luckily we're more enlightened now.

Lou: Why don't we look at what people are keeping for themselves and then get a general overview of what we're dealing with. It's just too abstract otherwise. There's a difference between a guitar and a watchstrap.

Varda: But how detailed are we going to get? Some things really are irrelevant. And by the way, don't think I haven't heard the snide comments about my red belt.

Martin: I move that we omit Varda's red belt from the list.

Gila: All right, let's start with a vote on whether to a) look at specific cases before deciding on the need for new guidelines, or b) try to come up with a formula first, based for example on whether the item could be useful to others, its value, its purpose …

Martin: Acquisition equals mass times the speed of envy squared.

Lou: Envy doesn't enter into it.

Dori

We're at Galron. I pick up a cardboard wheel that teaches you how to read with dots. I turn the wheel and look at the different dots. I could learn it now if I wanted to. But what's the rush?

A new girl joined our Group today. Her name is Hannah. She's very tall with white skin and long blonde hair that she doesn't want to braid or put in an elastic. She doesn't have a mother and I think her father is a dentist. He'll have to do things aside from fixing teeth because most people's teeth don't need fillings more than once a year. It's different with Dafna because there's always someone who's sick.

Hannah isn't a Pioneer and she doesn't want to be one. She doesn't like Eldar and she doesn't like us. I tried to talk to her but she didn't answer me.

Diary of a Young Man

6 February 1922. There is still much that is missing from our commune; we don't even have a clothing pool yet. People hesitate to share in this area.

8 February 1922. Finally, there is a clothing pool.

At the moment it's not mandatory, but most members were enthusiastic, and immediately a procession of suitcase-bearers formed in the yard, marching towards the storage area next to the kitchen.

There are those, however, who oppose the pool. In our Meetings, they argue that it's too early, we haven't yet created the necessary conditions—that is, intensive, communal life that is broad and profound. When those conditions are reached, the pool will come into being naturally.

Dori

Hannah has a different way of drawing the sky. Instead of one blue line on top she fills the whole space with light blue. And instead of pressing her crayons she makes everything pale. Like her.

I don't know about not pressing but I have to admit that her sky is better. We want to copy her but we don't like her so we pretend we don't like her sky.

I asked Daddy if he could trace the beautiful gas station picture from the black book of paintings. He said he could! And he's doing it! It's going to take him a long time because it's a very hard picture.

I'm so happy he's tracing it! I'm going to have a copy all my own. I'm very lucky with my Daddy.

Landscape with Garage Lights, by Naftali

Dori

Another wonderful Hike with Carmella.

Some of the children are saying that if you cut a worm in half it becomes two worms. They find a worm and cut it in half and both parts start to move. But I don't think the worm likes it. I don't think there are two worms now. I hope they won't do it again.

Suddenly I find a *rakefet* hiding under a boulder! *Wondrous and dainty, with wings like a fairy's*—the song is exactly right. Delicate white with a tiny bit of dark pink at the bottom and then slowly turning into white. Oh I'm going to burst with happiness. I lie on my stomach and look and look. If only I could do more than look. That's the problem with everything. All you can do is look.

Baby Diary

December 1.
Crawling *backwards*.

Dori

We had a letter from Jonathan. Shoshana read it to us. He said he likes his new kibbutz and he has a tricycle.

We're all jealous. He's a show-off.

He doesn't miss us at all.

As a matter of fact I had a tricycle in Canada. I rode it all the way to the corner store and back. My brother David was raking the leaves with a boy who lived next door who always had a Band-Aid on his knee. A boy Daddy didn't like but we played with him anyhow. I bought two pink popsicles at the store and when I came back the leaves were in a big pile and we jumped on them and ate our popsicles. A half for me a half for David and a half for the boy with the Band-Aid and a half for his little sister Louise.

Our First Year

24 July 1949. A big celebration in honour of Eldar's first child, Avital. Indeed none of us, aside from the parents and one or two privileged individuals, has yet seen the infant (who must be protected from the microbes of ordinary mortals), nor was she able to participate in the large-scale festivities in her honour.

Eli even composed a song for the occasion to words by Edna. Archie delivered a lecture, with props, on the Care and Feeding of Infants, in which he explained the phenomenon of "leaking" in the young child—nothing surprising, he assured us, in view of the fact that the human being consists mainly of water.

Dori

It's Hanukkah.

After supper we go to the Dining Hall and walk in the dark holding candles and singing Candle My Candle and We Come to Dispel the Dark. They're both beautiful songs.

What I like best is when we sing—

> We come to dispel the dark
> With our candles glowing bright
> Each one a tiny flame
> Together a great light

Because it isn't just a song. It's what we're really doing. That doesn't happen usually.

Dispelling the Dark

Dori

We have to rush in the morning now that we're going to Galron.

But by mistake Shoshana brought a soft-boiled egg for me from the Kitchen instead of hard. She says *you're just going to have to eat it.* But I can't eat a soft-boiled egg. I'll throw up.

Shoshana says *no one is leaving until Dori eats her egg.* I start to cry but she won't give in. I cry right into the egg. I move it with my fork but I can't eat it. It doesn't even look like food.

I cry and cry and Shoshana gets angrier and angrier.

Finally she tells me to take the bowl with me and eat the egg on the walk to the microbus. I hold the bowl and the fork and walk and cry. Suddenly I have an idea. I spill the egg in the bushes.

I tell Shoshana I finished and give her the bowl. I tricked her.

Between the Motion and the Act

Rubin changed the subject: "What do you have against your wife?"

"What exactly do you mean?"

"Why do you torment her for no reason?"

"You really think so?"

"Are you kidding? Sometimes you act as if she's your slave. She's afraid to say the wrong thing at the wrong time at the wrong place. What do you do to scare her so much? It's not her fault that I look at her—I can't help it. And what's wrong with that, why shouldn't I? I don't see you stopping yourself from looking at Esther or Brauna or anyone else. Free her, free her!"

"Do you really think so?" Nat repeated, both repelled by and appreciating Rubin's honesty, knowing he was only partly right, partly wrong.

Dori

Hannah sits with me on the patio of the Children's House. The patio is my favourite part of Eldar. The floor is made of big purple tiles in different shapes that curve into each other. Even when it's hot the tiles are cold if your feet are bare or if you lie down and put your cheek on them. I want to eat those tiles.

We once got our hair washed with kerosine on the patio. Dafna came to help Shoshana. We took off all our clothes except for our underwear and Dafna told us to close our eyes really tight while she put the kerosene in our hair. The kerosene was in a big rusty barrel. I like that word—barrel.

After we washed our hair with the kerosene Shoshana sprayed us with water from a hose. We ran in and out of the water and went wild. It was fun.

Hannah has a soft voice. Maybe she's only shy. She says *I'll think of a number from one to ten and you have to guess it.* I guess *three* and she shakes her head. Then she says *you're allowed to lie in this game.*

The game makes absolutely no sense to me but I don't care. I'm happy that Hannah's finally talking to me.

But then suddenly she gets up and walks away. She really hates Eldar.

Diary of a Young Man

14 February 1922. The Meeting yesterday was profound. We spoke—actually only one spoke, and the others were silent—about Eros in society, about individual freedom. I didn't understand most of it, but the discussion was imbued with a special spirit that can't be put into words. It is no wonder that Eros is central to our talks—we bare our souls before one another.

20 February 1922. I am still shattered from yesterday's discussion. Some time after midnight I was startled out of a deep sleep by the clanging of the bell. I was sure that our camp was in flames. Half-naked, I ran outside, but all was quiet—no sign or hint of a fire.

I approached the others, who were emerging from their tents, and asked them in a fearful voice where the fire was. But they reassured me and in hushed tones told me to keep my voice down, for the bell was summoning us to a Meeting. I wondered why a Meeting was being called at midnight. I returned to my tent, dressed, and made my way to the Dining Hall [mess tent].

The tent was half in darkness and somewhere in a corner a small lamp flickered. On the floor, against the walls, people sat huddled together, and from one of the corners, as if rising from the depths, came the voice of Y.B. like the voice of a spirit, full of mystery. The speaker kept his head bowed, and disembodied words broke through the dim space.

"I called for a talk (long silence) ... because I ... that is, we, every individual (long silence) ... The society, one family (long silence)."

All the comrades sat with their heads bowed, their faces concealed. I rested my chin on my knees and listened. The rest of the Meeting eluded me, because I fell asleep in my dark corner.

The guard who came to light the Primus for tea woke me. Too bad I fell asleep. I was told that there never was such a beautiful and profound Meeting.

Dori

Daddy brings me a pair of slippers from the city. The same blue slippers with a zipper on the side and white fur on top but new.

Because last week he noticed my slippers in the Children's House. He looked at them and said angrily *are these your slippers?* He was disgusted that they were falling apart. I don't know why. I like falling-apart slippers.

As soon as he leaves everyone decides to hate me. It's my turn to be hated. Every child gets a turn it seems.

When it was Skye we all sang—

> *Hanan and Elsa went out to the field*
> *Hanan was the shepherd and Elsa the sheep*
> *Meh meh meh meh meh meh*
> *Meh meh meh meh meh meh*

It's supposed to be Hanan and Aliza but we changed it because Skye's parents are called Hanan and Elsa. Skye acted like she didn't care. I don't know if she was pretending or if she really didn't care.

Now everyone sings—

The sun is shining gold and red
Naftali has a big bald head

instead of—

The sun is shining gold and red
And plum trees blossom overhead

but it doesn't hurt me because there's nothing wrong with being bald. Being hated hurts me but not the song about Daddy. Even being hated isn't so bad. It's because of the slippers.

After our shower when I go to put on my new slippers there's a squished banana inside. They finally hurt me.

Shoshana cleans the banana out with a rag and tells us to get into bed.

I didn't even want new slippers.

Late Night Confessions

"By age eleven we were so wild and out of control that it became a game with us, seeing how long it would take for our latest Minder to lose it. We celebrated when we finally succeeded. We drove one Minder after another to a nervous breakdown."

—Yair Miron

Dori

It's getting cold at night. We have grey blankets to keep us warm.

Mummy comes to kiss me goodnight. I tell her about the banana in my slipper and she says *I'm sorry* as if it's her fault.

She does that a lot. On the ship there was a storm and we all began to throw up. It was the fault of the waves but Mummy kept saying *I'm sorry*.

Another time it really was her fault but it was a mistake. I had a cold and Mummy put medicine from a blue jar on my chest. But she didn't know the medicines in Canada and she put too much and my chest began to burn as if I had a fire in there. I kept yelling *water water* and she kept running to bring me more water saying *I'm sorry I'm sorry* but it was a mistake.

Just before Sara was born Mummy burnt both her hands. She forgot a pot was hot and she put her hands around it. The doctor gave her cream that looked like throw-up and she lay in bed with the cream on her hands and a blue lamp on her leg. My brother David pinched his nose and said *ugh that looks like throw-up.* He ran into Mummy's bedroom from the door on one side of her bed and out the door on the other side of her bed saying *ugh ugh* and pinching his nose. It was funny so I began running too saying *ugh ugh* and pinching my nose and then we both ran in circles around Mummy's bed laughing and pinching our nose and Mummy laughed too. Finally Daddy told us to stop because Mummy had to rest.

There was a rainstorm when Mummy went to the hospital to have Sara. Daddy had to hold the umbrella for Mummy so she could get to the taxi without getting wet but the wind ruined the umbrella. I saw it all from the living-room window. So I wasn't surprised when they brought the baby back from the hospital and said her name was Sara.[52]

Our First Year

17 August 1949. Our Arab agricultural advisor from Kitlish was here today, looking over our vines and advising us when and how to harvest.

Dori

Shoshana says we have to line up for a teaspoon of cod liver oil and then we'll get a candy.

We don't want to line up. We have a bad feeling about this cod liver oil.

When my turn comes I can't even believe that anything so horrible exists in this world. I feel I'm going to throw up but I grab the candy and put it in my mouth.

The candy doesn't help Elan. He swallows the cod liver oil and right away he throws up. Shoshana gets mad and makes him take it again and he throws up again.

Now Shoshana's really angry. She gives it to him a third time. He still throws up. There's less throw-up this time because there isn't a lot left in his stomach.

I feel bad for Elan. Very bad. But Shoshana hates him. She hates all of us but she hates him the most.

Shoshana says we have to have cod liver oil every day now. I don't understand it. Eldar is supposed to be nice to children.

Thy Neck with Chains of Gold

RIVKA   Ricky doesn't believe in my Polish cousin.

MICHAEL   Do you care what Ricky thinks?

RIVKA   He said people are talking.

MICHAEL   Is that why you didn't come into town this week?

RIVKA   No. I wasn't able to get a day off. *(She breaks away from him)* Michael, I'm pregnant. Michael—let's get out of here. We'll go away—back to America—and we'll be together, in the open. No more hiding.

MICHAEL   You're not serious? Look, Rivka, I've no intention of ever going back.

RIVKA   It's not so bad there. You had bad luck—but now it'll change.

MICHAEL   If it's so great there, why did you leave?

RIVKA   I ... believed.

MICHAEL   I believed too.

RIVKA   I grew up with *Israel* on my lips. But maybe now we've done our duty. They can get along without us. No one is indispensable.

MICHAEL   I fought for this country and now that it's ours I won't leave it. It's also mine, you understand—mine. And I'm going to die here, Rivka. *(Pause)* The other day I climbed the mountain and picked the spot where they'll bury me. I planted four little trees to shade my grave. They need time to grow. I have to stick around. This is my home.

RIVKA   All right, we'll stay. We'll move to the city—

MICHAEL   But I like it here.

RIVKA   What do you like about it? You drive the truck to get away.

MICHAEL   I've been thinking ... I want to start a high school here in Eldar, for our children and children from the poorest neighbourhoods in the country. I've seen them on my trips, living in hovels, barely enough to eat. We can bring them here and teach them, give them a chance.

RIVKA   Then we'll stay here and you'll leave Marina.

MICHAEL   Why?

RIVKA   Michael, don't you love me?

Dori

I'm alone in the Children's House. Suddenly I notice Skye's necklace. The one with the gold heart. It's in a little box on her bed. A pretty blue box.

I take the bracelet outside and dig a hole in the ground and bury it.

It's not a very nice thing to do. Skye is going to miss that bracelet.

I can tell her where I buried it if she asks. I didn't throw it out.

I have some things that are only mine—like the little doll furniture on the tray. But I keep them in the Room. I don't bring them to the Children's House where everyone can see them and be jealous.

Our First Year

30 August 1949. We began the grape harvest yesterday. Some of the fruit is inferior, but there are many bunches that hang like clusters of monstrous jewels, succulent grapes the size of small plums, beautifully formed, with a powdery bloom that rubs off leaving an enamelled surface, shiny and sometimes pitch black.

Dori

Skye's been asking about her bracelet. I want to tell her where it is but the problem is that I forgot where I buried it.

Diary of a Young Man

18 March 1922. Sometimes you're lying in bed, thinking about the commune, and suddenly you hear the sound of weeping. You get up and step outside to help your comrade in distress. But next to the tent where the sound is coming from several young women have gathered and they gesture to you, "Don't come near!" They're watching and helping. There are already quite a few experts in hysteria.

Dori

We're at Galron and we're having a problem. Carmella doesn't know we're here and there's a dog barking in front of the door. He looks dangerous.

We're afraid to go into the yard. Shoshana's afraid too. We keep waiting for Carmella but she doesn't come.

Finally Skye decides to be brave. She goes into the yard and walks sideways very very slowly. She keeps her back to the fence and then to the wall.

But the dog jumps on her and bites her. She screams and Carmella comes out. Skye is screaming her head off. Carmella puts her on a chair and gives her a candy and one of the children gives her a toffee and another child gives her a ribbon.

I want to give her something too. I have a boat in my pocket that I found yesterday on our Hike. It's a teeny-tiny red boat and I decided I would keep it until I was old and bent with a shawl so I'd have something from when I was a little girl.

But Skye is crying and all I have is the boat so I give it to her. She takes it but she goes on crying.

Finally the nurse comes running in. She gives Skye a shot in her arm. Poor Skye! She was brave and she got bit and had to get a shot. In stories brave people end up with the prize but not in real life apparently.

Between the Motion and the Act

They sat at the table, singing apathetically in order to postpone the main event of the evening: a lottery to determine which two members would join the army on a dangerous mission the following morning. The army had asked for two men and the members had decided on a lottery. The tension grew as each of the men took a small piece of paper out of a hat. Two were marked.

Nat thought of the scene in Charlie Chaplin's The Great Dictator, in which the Resistance puts coins in a pudding to select someone to go on a suicide mission to assassinate the dictator, and each person tries to hide the coin and secretly pass it on. As he opened his paper he contemplated what might be on it. They had arrived here only a few months ago, knowing that war was imminent. Most of them had fought in World War Two in the Canadian and U.S. armies, and were dismayed by the thought that they'd have to go through it all again. But duty and love of the country were the order of the day—and what were they if not the innocent sons of the era?

Nat's piece of paper was spread out on the table now but he did not have the courage to look at it. He was not afraid of dying, of suffering, of being killed, but he dreaded the thought of leaving Avra—blonde, beautiful, flowering, and as mysterious as a Japanese opera; to be torn apart from her now—perhaps lose her forever—that was what he was afraid of. He looked at the other men in the room, and concluded that his own paper was not marked, for Rubin rose with feigned abhorrence and smiled, and his wife tried to be brave and smile too. Everyone felt somewhat relieved, for Rubin was considered indefatigable, an ex-Air Force Pilot who had been awarded a Silver Star. He would surely return, there was no doubt about it.

The second person whose paper was marked was Pinny. He went pale, and his blue eyes began to water. His wife moaned by his side, "Pinny, no!"

They felt sorry for Pinny and in spite of their previous resolution, they accepted Samuel's offer to go in Pinny's place. Samuel was not really one of them. He was a Brazilian who had come on his own. He was drawn into the enthusiastic devotion of the group; nevertheless, when he was killed on a lone hill in the Negev, he was barely mourned. When Pinny heard about it, all he said was, "What luck! It could have been me."

Dori

Now that it's colder we're getting shirts with long sleeves. I really like this one red shirt with a high neck. It's very soft. I'm not supposed to get a shirt just because I like it because what if the other children like it just as much?

But Shoshana gave it to me last time and again this time. It's not what I expect from Shoshana but what do you know—she was nice for a change.

I like the shirt but I don't like anything touching my throat. Even at night I sleep with my hand on my throat so the blanket won't touch it.

I keep the neck of the shirt in my mouth so it won't touch my throat. Just like Bazooka Joe. I wonder if he's like me. Maybe he can't have anything touching his throat either.

Baby Diary

January 1, 1956
Had a smallpox shot. I handed over the 10:00 nursing to the Minder. Gets food and a cup (no bottle). Niv, Simon and Dori have moved to new quarters next to the Baby House.

Weaning was very hard for me. (Emotionally.)

She is fine—a happy, sweet, pretty and good girl.

Dori

Mummy is baking a cake in the Room. I'm helping her whip the whites.

When Carmella baked a cake she whipped the whites so hard that when she turned the bowl upside-down they didn't fall out. Even with gravity.

So when the whites are ready I turn the bowl upside-down to show Mummy. I say *look it's standing*! but suddenly the whole thing slides down to the floor in one big piece.

Mummy is very upset but not angry. She finds a way to save most of the egg whites and she puts them back in the bowl. Daddy comes in and she tells him what happened. When she gets to the part where I said *it's standing* Daddy bursts out laughing and Mummy laughs too and they repeat *it's standing* over and over and they laugh so hard that tears come out of Mummy's eyes.

It's nice when you make your parents laugh. A bad thing turned into a good thing.

Kibbutz Cake

Dori

It's Tu B'shvat Festival of Trees today. I love Tu B'shvat. We wear white shirts and everyone plants a tree. An adult helps me dig a hole and I put the sapling in the earth and I pat the earth back in. Pat pat pat.

Everyone is happy. There are hundreds of yellow and white wildflowers around us. The beautiful wildflowers of our land. I love our land.

Report Card

Government of Palestine
DIRECTORATE OF EDUCATION

SCHOOL The Amiriya School in Jish

CLASS Seventh

SCHOOL YEAR 1946

STUDENT'S NAME Muhammad Abdullah Edgaim

STUDENT'S AGE 14 years, 4 months

RANK First

AVERAGE AGE OF STUDENTS IN HIS CLASS 14 years, 11 months

NUMBER OF STUDENTS IN THE CLASS Fifteen

SUBJECT	RANK	TEACHERS' OBSERVATIONS
[illegible]	First	
Arabic language	Second	Very good. —Atanasius 'Aql
English language	Third	Very good. —Atanasius 'Aql
Arithmetic and geometry	Fourth	
History and geography	First	Very good. —Atanasius 'Aql
Principles of science	First	Very good, smart, diligent, determined.
Drawing and manual training		

CLASS TEACHER'S OBSERVATIONS:

Hard-working, diligent. His morals are good. —Hassan Abdul Hussein

PRINCIPAL'S OBSERVATIONS:

Hard-working and diligent. Good luck for the first year of secondary school.

Dori

I don't know where we are. All I know is that we're in Meron and the room is very crowded. We're supposed to get sandwiches but I don't know where. I can't see anyone from my Group or anyone else from Eldar.

I find a girl to talk to. An old girl—almost ten. She's from Meron. She says *I have a rabbit called Fifi.* I tell her about the dog that bit Skye.

Finally Shoshana comes to get me and we all leave Meron in a bus. It's dark outside. Shoshana says we have to go straight to the Children's House and to bed.

I say *I have to tell Daddy or Mummy we're back.* But Shoshana says it's too late.

I feel sick. I can't go to sleep without a goodnight kiss. So when Shoshana isn't looking I run away as fast as I can to the Room. There's no one there so I run to the Kitchen. But Daddy isn't there either and no one knows where he is. Someone says Mummy might be in Coco's Room.

So I start running back to the Rooms but Shoshana comes running down the path and catches me. She grabs my waist and carries me screaming back to the Children's House.

I try to stop crying but I can't. My crying is like hiccups. No matter what I do I can't make it stop. Shoshana laughs *listen to her hiccup.* She wants everyone to laugh with her.

I know Daddy or Mummy would come if they knew I was back. But they don't know and there's no one to tell them.

This is the saddest anyone can be. It isn't possible to be sadder than this.

Transcript of Meeting
February 1962

Topic: Improvisational Cuisine
Chair: Isaac Milman

Isaac: We're a small group today because several of our comrades are working extra hours setting up the new library,
and some are away at the Federation seminar. Edna is
concerned about: "Rumours that some of our meat last
week came from a wild boar caught by our comrades. I
commend the Kitchen on its valiant efforts to keep us
fed and its excellent culinary skills, but I don't think it's
safe to eat wild animals, especially for our children."

Naftali: We really took every precaution, boiling the meat for
hours. After all, humans have been hunting and cooking meat for millions of years.

Tamir: What about the fuel required to boil the meat for hours?
Does it really make economic sense in the end?

Naftali: If you want to live on borscht it's fine with me. If you
want omelettes, on the other hand, we may have to crack
a few eggs.

Edna: I know our policy is children first—but in this case, I suggest that with anything experimental, we stick to adults.

Tamir: And if the adults don't die, we can give it to the kids.

Martin: How long should we wait to see if the adult dies?

Naftali: We'll go by weight. Skinny people, three days. Fat people,
a week.

Martin: While we're on the subject, I haven't seen soup bits on
the table in three weeks.

Edna: They're going to the Children's Houses. The kids love
them.

Naftali: We could plan a midnight raid on Osem headquarters.
Anyone know where they're located?

Martin: The army won't release that information. Torture has
been attempted, without results.

Naftali:	We'll have to infiltrate.
Isaac:	Much as I'm enjoying the jocularity of our comrades, I suggest we address Edna's concern. Let's vote on whether to restrict meat from improvised sources to adults. It's not like we're desperate—our food situation has improved over the past few years.
Martin:	That's true. We've moved from shoe leather to sardines.
Isaac:	Who's in favour of restricting meat for the children to certified sources?
Vote:	For: 11 Abstentions: 1

Dori

Today I'm the luckiest girl on Eldar. Daddy did something he's not really supposed to do. We were talking about the sandwiches I didn't get in Meron and Daddy took me to the Kitchen and poured a huge amount of soup bits into a pot and he gave me the pot. The whole pot! I couldn't believe my eyes.

I wander off in the direction of the barns. I don't want to meet anyone. We almost never get soup bits and when we do we're only allowed one spoon each.

And now I have a whole pot to myself. A whole pot!

I wander to the barns eating my soup bits. I don't meet anyone. I walk and eat. This is a happy day. Better even than a birthday.

Our First Year

9 September 1949. The First Rain has arrived. Clouds piled up like a dark flotilla and cruised over the Atzmon mountain range, and then very unexpectedly a few drops began to fall on the grape leaves and drop from the fruit like tears.

In the course of the day there were sudden drenching out-
bursts and the wind blasted away. There was mud and the smell
of wetness.

Tomorrow we expect to put 30 people in the field to finish off
the grape harvest. Meanwhile the figs grow larger and juicier.

The main topic of discussion these days is "elections." The
administrative and committee positions in the kibbutz are
reshuffled at this time of the year, and the process is complicated
and yields heated controversy. Our big problem is to find a general
manager and a secretary. Nobody wants the honours.

Dori

There was a movie for everyone today. It was about a boy
and his bull. I didn't understand most of it but at the end
the bull got shot with arrows and the boy couldn't get
there on time. It was very sad. The arrows hit the bull and
stayed in his skin and he was bleeding but the man kept
shooting more and more arrows in him. The bull tried to
escape but he couldn't. I began crying so hard that someone had to take me out of the Dining Hall.

In some places shooting arrows into bulls is a sport
and everyone cheers. Some people care about bulls and
some people don't.[53]

Our First Year

11 September. This seems to be the season of gremlin wounds,
those tiny, unserious lesions and abrasions that pop out on the
body in the course of the day's work: a blood blister here, a scraped
area here, a scratch, an opening, a puncture there.

A collection of these little beauty spots can upset one's dispos-
ition quite seriously.

You can't move this finger, must remember not to bend that elbow in such an angle, the foot can't be exposed in this position, don't sit on that particular spot on the left buttock, can't allow the left lower palm to touch anything, etc.

They appear mysteriously, these clotted, discoloured, swollen, scaly, or rashlike decorations; they metamorphose continually, persisting against all kind of balms and smears and bandages.

It may be the climate, the season, the dust, or a kind of juvenile delinquency in the department of providential retribution.

Dori

My brother David is reading about a trickster called Till Eulenspiegel. He plays all sorts of tricks on people. The tricks are funny. In one story he goes to sleep in a bee-hive and when two thieves steal the beehive he pulls their hair and they begin to fight because each thief thinks the other thief is pulling his hair.

Till Eulenspiegel does things for a reason. The reason is that people are bad.

David sometimes does things for no reason. One time in Canada David was looking after me and he saw that when I made a poo I checked the toilet paper to see when it was clean. He began to laugh and make fun of me. I didn't know it was a stupid thing to do.

Then Daddy called on the phone. And David said *do you know what Dori does—when she wipes herself she looks at the paper* and he began to laugh. I began to yell *no no* and I ran to the phone and grabbed it from David and said *it isn't true it isn't true* but I knew it was too late and that Daddy would know it was true.

Why did David have to tell him? He just did it to be mean. Just like that.

Complicated Procedures

Dori

Shoshana takes us on a short Hike to see bees. Usually Shoshana's Hikes are boring but the bees are interesting. Coco looks after the hives. She wears a special hat with a net and special clothes that bees can't sting through.

Even with the hat and the clothes I'd be scared. But Coco is brave. She smiles at us and tries to explain what she's doing but no one listens. We like the bees and the hives and Coco's special hat but we're a bit worried about getting stung.

Shoshana's scared too. She laughs a little but she's scared.

Another thing about Coco apart from her shaggy dog and the bees is that she planted a whole bed of Amnon-and-Tamar flowers.[54] I think I have to add Amnon-and-Tamar to my favourite flowers. Each flower has two colours—yellow and purple or light purple and dark purple. And they all look like velvet. Every time I see them I'm surprised that you can plant something so beautiful.

Coco is a good person to have on Eldar.

Diary of a Young Man

29 March 1922. A full moon—spring is here—yesterday we sat on the boulders and sang. The whole commune gathered together without the ringing of the bell, and everyone sang and sang—suddenly without knowing how or why, a circle came into being and the commune began to dance. We danced for hours without pause. Our legs rose on their own, shoulder adjoining shoulder, the entire commune poured into one great soul and danced.

2 April 1922. We do not cease to speak of the dance of that night. Will such a dance ever come again?

20 April 1922. Unbelievable, what those moshav [community of cooperative farms] people are capable of! Simply boggles the mind!

In the middle of today's dance, at the height of our fervour and sense of closeness, a few moshav people who happened to be in the Dining Hall burst into the circle.

Instantly our singing ceased and we all left the circle, leaving the moshav people alone in the middle of the tent. And thus our celebration was cut short. What's really interesting is that they don't understand what ails us.

How can they not comprehend—the commune's dance is an internal event, like the commune's Meeting, and a stranger cannot have any part of it.

Dori

Daddy can touch the tip of his nose with his tongue. That's very hard to do. He also has a gold tooth.

I can stand on my head up to 100 if I have a pillow and it's near a wall.

My brother David can move his ears. He's the only person on Eldar who can do that. He also knows Everybody Loves Saturday Night in six languages. There was a talent show on the ship from Canada and he got up on stage and sang that song in all six languages.

I don't know what Mummy can do.

Our First Year

2 October 1949. I think back now to the earlier months of the year, when we looked with such wonderment and anticipation at the clean fig trees with their hard, green knobs popping out like buttons at the ends of the branches, when we kept trying to conjure forth the taste and shape of the ripe fruit.

Now those little green knobs attack our eyes as heaps of yellow, split, spoiling fruit, and behind each yellow conidial blotch leers the image of an ideologically compromised Arab. The stuff was ripening, splitting, falling, and terrifying us by the ton (the fig harvest is a countrywide problem), but now we've got the situation under control.

Dori

The older children are picking peas. We can pick too if we want but we aren't really supposed to eat the peas because they're for selling to people outside of Eldar. It's hard to resist though. Peas straight from the pod are delicious.

The older children tell us to go play. I run around with Lulu and then I go to the Room. Daddy isn't there. No one's there. I go back down to look for him. Coco opens her window and says Daddy can't see me today because he has a bad back.

And Mummy went away for two days to a conference! Daddy was all I had!

I sit on the step and cry my heart out. I have the same feeling I had last time when Shoshana caught me and the same hiccups when I try to stop. My whole heart is breaking and my stomach too. There's no one to take me to the Children's House so finally Shoshana comes and drags me.[55]

In years to come, I shall be glad to be unwept, unchallenged and unsung. Farewell, dust! Farewell, Eldar!

Dori

One thing I do not like is steam houses. On the beach in Camp Bilu'im there was a steam house on the beach. I wasn't allowed in there but I begged and begged and in the end David let me in. I sat on a bench in a tiny room. The smell made me sick and the steam made me sick. I yelled *let me out!* And I ran out and never went in there again.

What I like is the tall brown stove in the Room in winter. It has little holes and you can put your cheek against the metal and warm up. It has a such nice smell.

I love the light inside a flashlight or any kind of light inside glass. I saw a red light inside glass here on Eldar but I never found out what it was. Light inside glass is magic and real at the same time.

Stove

Dori

Mummy is taking me to the city! Just the two of us all day long. She says she has a surprise for me there.

A lot of Arab women get on the bus with their baskets. Mummy laughs every time the bus bumps because it makes us jump up in our seats. I laugh with her. She peels an orange and gives me half because we left before breakfast. She says *pelah*[56] *pelah Metushelah* which doesn't mean anything—it just rhymes. Usually words that don't mean anything are for babies but everyone says *pelah pelah Metushelah*. Even my brother David.

Mummy has to go to an office. It takes a long time. I play with my sunhat but there isn't much you can do with a sunhat. When we're finished Mummy says *you were so patient!* I say *I wasn't patient at all* and she laughs very hard. I don't know why exactly.

We go to a toilet to pee because later there might not be a toilet. It isn't very clean but Mummy brought pieces of newspaper in her purse and she puts them on the seat so we won't catch any germs. Then we wash our hands with soap. Mummy says *with soap you don't have to worry who touched it.*

On the street I see a woman with very puffed hair. I say, *look Mummy she has a cake on her head!* and Mummy says *shhh* so the woman won't hear but she smiles. She says *now I have a surprise for you—we're going to see a Tarzan movie.*

I can't believe it! Now I'm the happiest girl in the world. The happiest girl who ever lived in the whole wide world.

We go into the cinema. The seats are made of wood and they bounce up unless you hold them. Mummy holds the seat down for me. It goes up a bit when I sit on it because I'm not heavy enough but I don't mind. The movie starts. First there's a monkey and then an elephant brings Tarzan a log. Then a boy sweeps the floor. He sweeps all the dirt under a carpet.

Mummy leans over and whispers *look how he sweeps!* So then I know it's a joke and I laugh.[57]

The boy is Tarzan's son. Mummy explains the movie to me but two big girls keep turning around to look at us and Mummy says we're bothering them.

I don't mind not understanding everything. It's still the best movie in the world with the handsomest man in the world.

When the movie is over Mummy says out loud *the end*. The sun outside hurts my eyes and I have to cover them. Mummy says *I think I'm ready for the beach!* This is turning out to be the best day of my life.

On the way to the beach Mummy sees some stairs going down. She's very curious about where they go. She says *should we go see where those stairs lead?* and I say *yes* and she says *but then we'll have to climb back up.* She decides to go down anyhow. So we go down but when we get to the bottom there are more stairs! She can't decide again.

Finally she decides to go down those stairs too. But when we get to the end there are even more stairs! Mummy says *well that's it* and we go back up without ever finding out what was there. She was right about going up. It's much harder than going down.

We walk to the beach and Mummy pays for a beach chair. She takes a bathing suit out of her bag and helps me put it on. She says *you can play in the water but stay on the foam* and she lies down on the chair and goes to sleep.

I sit on the soft foam and feel it with my fingers. I let the waves go over my legs. I look out at the sea and get the *abracadabra* feeling. That huge feeling of longing for something in the future. The longing makes me think of the song—

Oh the deep blue of the sea
Jerusalem I long for thee

Only the beginning of the song is beautiful. Then it changes and gets stupid.

I dig holes in the wet sand and collect pretty shells. I shake the shells in my hands. My favourites are the twisty ones with the pointy edge. I love the beach.

A man comes by yelling *Artik Artik*. He has a big box tied to his neck. Mummy wakes up and asks for two lemon Artiks. Lemon Artiks are much better than the popsicles in Canada. They're softer and sweeter and more lemony. You have to eat them fast though. Otherwise they fall apart and drip on everything.

Mummy looks at her watch and says *we have to go back*. She isn't happy about going back. I take off my bathing suit and get dressed. Mummy sings—

To Israel we came
Because we're insane

and I laugh. The song is supposed to be—

To Israel we came
To plant and sow grain

Mummy laughs with me. We laugh all the way to the bus.

Diary of a Young Man

25 May 1922. An event perpetrated by the "Night Group" yesterday stirred up a great deal of anger among some of our families. When they woke up in the morning they saw the hut of the empty Children's House, which we have just built, had been rearranged to resemble the room of a petit-bourgeois family: two neatly made beds with slippers placed beneath them; on the husband's bed a pipe and various accessories typical of a petit-bourgeois family room.

The message is clear: families are beginning to isolate themselves from the life of the greater family—the commune.

Strong feelings have been aroused, and the behaviour of the "Night Group" is being labelled tactless, truly brutish! R. even cried at this piece of mischief.

15 June 1922. Our road work has ended and we have been moved to Nahalal to drain malaria-producing swamps. The hammer and chisel have been replaced by picks and shovels, highly unromantic tools.

Our work is so demanding that our Meetings are taken up entirely by discussions related to work. It can be quite boring. Isn't it enough that we have to work all day, do we also have to discuss it at night?

But there are those among us, not many, for whom matters of work and economics are more important than the internal social life of the commune.

16 June 1922. For a while there have been rumours that some members consider a few other members unsuited to the commune.

Yesterday at the Meeting this rumour was brought out into the open by way of one person's demand that 48 members be asked to leave, of our total of 80—among them founders of the commune who have been here since its inception.

He listed the 48 members. There was a big hue and cry and his suggestion was condemned, even though secretly there are those who support him. Thus the 48 are staying and now divisiveness has been created. Altogether, this member has extraordinary ideas.

Dori

Hang down your head Tom Dooley!
Hang down your head and cry!
Hang down your head Tom Dooley!
Poor boy you're bound to die!

Met her on the mountain!
There I took her life!
Met her on the mountain!
Stabbed her with my knife!

Hang down your head Tom Dooley!
Hang down your head and cry!
Hang down your head Tom Dooley!
Poor boy you're bound to die!

Thy Neck with Chains of Gold

MICHAEL You want to know something, Rita—there is no love—only dreams, infatuations, and sex. The day you want to kill yourself for someone, you'll know it's love, and there's no one in this whole damn world I want to die for. So I may as well be married to Marina. She's good for me. There's only one thing worth giving your life for, and that's an ideal. An ideal you can shape and control. But people—are nothing. They betray you from the day you're born.

Dori

I'm putting on my socks next to Gilead's bed. He shows me a razor blade. He says his father gave it to him even though I thought he didn't have a father but maybe he does. He says *my father uses it for shaving.* He says *razors don't hurt when they cut you* and I say *I don't believe you* and he says *want to bet?* I say *ok.* We shake hands and do Abraham Isaac Jacob and he cuts the leg that doesn't have the sock on yet.

Blood comes pouring out! I scream and Shoshana comes and takes me over to the window and wraps a bandage around my leg but the blood goes right through the bandage. I'm screaming my head off.

167

Shoshana finds someone to carry me to the Room. Daddy and Mummy come in and kiss me but I'm still screaming. Dafna the nurse comes in and gives me a needle like Skye had when the dog bit her. Daddy asks me if I want a candy and I nod. I suck on the candy and feel better. More people come into the Room and leave.

Daddy says *we're calling the doctor to see if he can come to Eldar but if he can't we'll have to go to the hospital in Safed.* I really really don't want to go to the hospital.

Mummy comes in and says the doctor can't come— we'll have to drive to Safed. I say *will you come with me?* and Daddy says *of course dollie we'll all come with you.*

We drive in the back seat of a truck. In Canada one time I was coming home with Mummy and suddenly we saw an ambulance. Right on Davaar Street. Mummy said *let's go see what's going on* and I said *no no don't go!* But she went anyhow and she said *oh no it's grandpa!* I didn't understand how it could be my grandfather when it could have been anyone. If only she'd listened to me! But it would have been my grandfather no matter what. So then we had to drive in the ambulance with my grandfather and when we got to the hospital Mummy found a phone on the wall and called Daddy. I began to cry and she turned to me and said in a very worried voice *what is it?* I was surprised that she was asking *what is it?* but I could see she felt bad and I didn't want to make her feel worse so I stopped crying.

I'm not crying now either. I'm happy to be with Mummy and Daddy in a truck. I'm sitting on Daddy's lap.

We get to the hospital. It's crowded with people on chairs and beds and it doesn't look very clean. Mummy says *this is where you were born.* It bothers me that she wasn't alone and that she gave birth in a dirty hospital.

Dafna the nurse pulls a curtain so no one can see us. The doctor is an old man. I say *just tell him not to put on anything that burns!* So Daddy tells the doctor even though he doesn't want to. Everyone tells me how good I am but I'm not good. I'm making sounds even though nothing burns and nothing hurts. I'm just making them so people will worry about me.

The doctor tells Daddy something and Daddy says *this is going to burn a little* and I say *all right* because they told me. It only burns for a second. Dafna leans over me so I won't see and she tells the doctor what to do.[58]

The doctor gives me seven stitches. We drive back and I fall asleep on Daddy's lap.

Daddy carries me to the Children's House. I wake up on the way.

I'm worried about Gilead. Who knows what Shoshana did to him? She must have hit him even harder than Lulu.

Everyone is quiet in the Children's House and I can tell it's because something horrible happened. Even though Gilead didn't do it on purpose. He thought it was safe.

Mummy and Daddy help me get into pyjamas. They kiss me goodnight and leave. No one says anything. It's never been this quiet in the Children's House.

The truth is it wasn't such a bad day. My parents stayed with me the whole time. The stitches didn't hurt and I like Dafna. My parents like her too. Everyone was nice to me.

I only feel bad about Gilead. And now he'll think I don't like him.

Our First Year

16 November 1949. The figs have dropped almost all their leaves; they are now a sooty grey network of reaching, pointing branches, the buds like sharpened little fingertips. The vines are almost barren, bent over the stakes, or spread out and exposed as if in defeat, seeming as old and angularly weather-beaten as the middle-aged Arab women.

Dori

It's Purim. I didn't want to be boring Queen Esther but that's what I am. I have a dress and a crown and Mummy puts lipstick on my lips.

All I can think about the whole time is not licking my lips. I'm afraid the lipstick is poison. Mummy comes over and says *do you want me to take the lipstick off?* I nod and she wipes it off with a handkerchief.

How did she know?

Ethnography

After we left I dreamed about Eldar for almost a year.[59]

Dori

We're seeing a play in Meron. Mummy came with her Group and I came with my Group but Mummy takes me to sit next to her so she can explain the play to me. It's very noisy with everyone finding their seats.

A boy and his little brother come over and show us their tickets. They have brown skin like Gilead and they look poor and scared. They're wearing shorts and they don't even have shoes on their feet—only dirty old flip-flops. The problem is that their tickets have the same number as our chairs. Mummy checks the numbers and says *go tell the man at the door that there's a mistake.*

But the brothers are too scared. I want Mummy to go talk to the man at the door because they're the children and she's the adult but she keeps saying *go—go to the man at the door.*

The boy and his brother don't move. Can't Mummy see they're scared? Now they'll have to stand for the whole play. But then the play starts and it's so funny and wonderful I forget about the brothers. It's the best play I've seen in my life.

I don't know what happened to the brothers. Mummy should have helped them.

Genesis

I created them in My image.

Dori

Edna the baby Minder calls me on my way to the Room. I go over to the gate of the yard and she asks me to keep an eye on the baby in the yard because she has to go inside for a minute.

I stand on one side of the gate and the baby sits on the other side. I decide to help him stand up. He only needs some help and then he'll see it's easy.

I reach through the gate and pull him up. He smiles and stands but as soon as I let go he falls down. I pull him up again but when I let go he falls again. Now he's not so happy. He starts to cry. He doesn't like being pulled up but I try one last time. I shouldn't try but I do. It bothers me that he's weak and can't protect himself from me. And now I feel a strange boom boom boom in my jinnie.

I don't know what's going on.

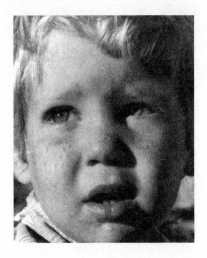

Dori

Our Children's House is getting rebuilt so we're moving to cabins at the edge of Eldar. In the cabins we have little tables next to our beds with a little drawer for small things like marbles.

They're also putting *zift* on the road today. It has a very strong smell and you mustn't touch it until it dries. I don't know if I like the smell or hate it. It's the same with horse manure. Do I like it or is it disgusting? I can't decide.

Actually I don't know if the stuff on the road is called *zift* or *zefet*. I'm a little confused about those words. *Zift* is definitely for when you don't think much of something.[60] Long ago a man visited Eldar and Daddy showed him around. The man said I was so pretty I could be Miss Israel when I grow up. After he left I asked Daddy what Miss Israel was and he said *zift*.

The only other time he said *zift* was when two men rolled on stage in Camp Bilu'im. It was an evening of plays. I was in the play that Daddy and Mummy put on. My brother David and I were supposed to sit at a table and run off when Daddy yelled at us and look scared but David laughed and that made me laugh.

After our play the curtain went up and there were two men wearing long robes lying on the stage hugging and rolling and making loud sounds and then the curtain went down. Everyone laughed. I asked Daddy why it was funny but he only said it was *zift*.

I don't care if Miss Israel is *zift* because I won't be Miss Israel anyway. Miss Israel sounds like something people in cities do. And Daddy says I won't be pretty because I'm ruining my teeth sucking my finger.

I don't know why the hugging men was *zift*.

Our First Year

2 December 1949. Surprising international incident occurred today. It seems that a U.N. committee is functioning on the border to straighten out some frontier questions between Israel and Lebanon. Attached to this committee were a number of Lebanese soldiers who apparently got lost and wandered onto our territory, whereupon they were immediately captured by Martin and brought to Eldar.

After some polite conversation in French we got things straightened out and sent the rather threadbare fellows back to Lebanon.[61]

Dori

We like the cabins a lot. Our beds are very close and we have those drawers. I don't need a goodnight kiss any more because all I have to do is stretch out my hand and I can touch the person next to me. And the end part of my bed touches the end part of Lulu's bed. We could touch each other's feet if we wanted.

Diary of a Young Man

15 February 1923. In a few months the number of our children will grow from one to four.

Among the soon-to-be mothers there are many discussions regarding childcare and education. It seems that there is some opposition to full collective childcare, especially handing over the washing of children to others.

These questions do not as yet have a place in the Meetings; it would surely be very strange if someone brought them to the Meeting. On the other hand, the opposition to collective child-care is also strange.

20 August 1923. Our commune has two new members—two children were born, a boy and a girl. The boy has been named Eitan and the girl Amira.

The more children, the more worries. We don't know how to look after four children at once. As long as we had only one child, no one was concerned. And now at every turn you meet worried mothers. The child isn't nursing, the child is nursing too much, is this good, is this bad? Who knows?

Who would have imagined that we would have four children and face such problems?[62]

Dori

Shoshana does the Wake-Up today. We want to run out as soon as we finish our snack but Lulu opens the door of the cabin and screams *snakes!* and shuts the door fast.

We all run to the window. There are two huge snakes outside on the slope. Really huge—longer than a person. They're twisted together like a braid.

We don't know what to do. I go to the door to make sure it's closed. Skye says the snakes are having sex but I don't see how. They're smooth all the way down.

So now we're stuck. Shoshana is afraid too. Finally Skye decides to be brave even though she got bit by a dog the last time she was brave. She opens the door and walks sideways along the wall of the cabin just like she did with the dog. When she gets to the top of the slope she runs as fast as she can.

We wait for her to call an adult. We wait and wait. Finally an adult comes and looks at the snakes. She puts her hands on her waist and then she goes away! Why didn't she save us?

One by one we do what Skye did. We slide next to the cabin and then run as fast as we can. I run all the way to the Room and I tell Daddy. I tell him the snakes are longer than the Room but he doesn't believe me and he doesn't want to come and see.

My brother David and No'am and Amnoni come with me to see the snakes. There are lots of children at the top of the slope now. Everyone is saying the snakes are rat snakes. Rat snakes aren't poisonous so we don't have to worry. Someone dares Amnoni to touch them. He runs down the slope and quickly touches one of them and then runs back up.

I could touch them too if I wanted. I'm not afraid because they're not poisonous. But in the end I don't.

Our First Year

4 December 1949. The tourists and visitors have been so thick we could start an Eldar branch of ambulatory Brooklyn Jewry. A very difficult problem is handling our guests appropriately. They pop in, stay for a few moments or an hour, and then push off, and in the brief interlude we want to give them some sort of understanding of Eldar. We often feel the futility of the process.

Yesterday I spent a precious two hours showing the place to a young couple from Baltimore. They were, it must be said, very sophisticated and very uninformed.

I tried to answer all their frequently very impolite questions, but it was obvious that they were envisioning everything in terms of certain streets and department stores and factories in Baltimore. "Friends," I wanted to shout at them, "you are touring a country which has been outside the stream of progressing civilisation for two thousand years, forget Baltimore!"

When they were standing near their 1949 Chrysler, ready to drive off, the young lady remembered a stock question that is asked in exams on Roman history, and sweetly inquired what "form of government" prevails here. This was the last straw. "Democratic anarchy," I said and went back to digging our new latrine.

Dori

I'm playing cards with Simon on his bed and he's losing. He looks so sad that I decide to give him the wild card. I put it face down on the bed so he can pick it up. He picks it up and he wins.

Then he starts boasting *I won I won!* He boasts to everyone.

Now I'm sorry I let him win.

It's Passover next week. The children Mummy teaches are putting on a play about Moses and Pharaoh. My brother David is going to be a slave.

Diary of a Young Man

25 September 1923. Departure! Today eleven members left at one go.

The unintelligent, as they proudly call themselves. They were constantly fuming, and in private discussions tried to prove that our commune was full of intellectual loafers, deluded dreamers, and that there's no room here for simple, hale workers with a positive attitude to labour.

Some say it's good they have left, as they didn't belong.

The commune lives on. There is a strong desire to overcome all obstacles. The weak will leave and the strong will stay.

1 January 1924. No work. The swamp-clearing was stopped and the stone-clearing has resulted in piles of stones that have no purpose.

We are cold and hungry. There's no work and no money. The wind rips our tents apart, leaving us exposed to the downpours and the mud. We spend the night at the bakery, where they make bread with flour that gets delivered from Haifa during the night. Homeless and tentless, felled by the wind, everyone comes to the warm bakery to enjoy a pita and a glass of black coffee without sugar. We stay all night. In the morning we put the tents back up.

Still, one by one, members are departing.

But what are these difficulties next to our celebrations? Our faith in the future of our commune has not diminished.

14 January 1924. Today, at the clothing stockpile, I was amazed to see a childcare worker taking underpants and undershirts into the Children's House. The woman explained that there are not enough diapers and underwear for the children, so they use those of the adults.

Dori

A magazine came in the mail from Mummy's friend in Canada. It has a booklet inside it with pictures of jewels on a black background. Pages and pages of pearls and rubies and diamonds on gold and on silver.

I don't know why Mummy's friend sent us this booklet. We can't buy any of these things and we also don't want to buy them because we don't believe in jewellery.[63]

I can't decide if I like the jewellery. It's very pretty but it's jewellery.

But here's something I know I like. Oh this is the most beautiful blue I have ever ever seen in my life. There's a girl in a big basket tied to a balloon and behind her is the most magnificent blue imaginable.

I cut the picture out and glue it on paper and now I can't stop looking at it. I'm going to keep this picture as long as I live.

Our First Year

25 December 1949. Yesterday afternoon about forty members rode off to Nazareth to hear the midnight mass choir. I stayed at home and worked in the kitchen, where I succeeded in giving the floor a good scrubbing.

After another crowd of fifteen or so went off to Jish to celebrate the holiday, we decided to have a little informal celebration of our own, so Yona prepared some toast spread with relish and tomato slices, and there was music and folk dancing and the small-crowd cozy feeling that weaves through the place whenever half the company departs.

On such occasions everyone sighs, "Oh, how nice it would be if we were a group of twenty or thirty," quietly forgetting that if such a tragic condition were to prevail they would go batty inside of a month. With a hundred people I imagine it will take us ten years to establish ourselves.

Dori

Carmella takes us to the forest to cook mushrooms for Lag B'omer. We're very excited. If only we had a Minder like Carmella everything would be different.

The forest has a heavenly smell and the ground is covered with pine needles and cones. We get wild but no one minds because it's a forest. The children from Galron tell us there's a baby buried in the forest. We go to look at the grave but all we see are some stones and no one knows if it's a grave or not.

Carmella has two helpers today. They make a bonfire and we collect mushrooms and they fry the mushrooms in a pan over the bonfire. They know which ones are safe to eat. Children aren't allowed to decide.

When the mushrooms are ready Carmella puts them on bread and hands the bread to anyone who wants. I take a bite but I don't really like the taste. The mushrooms are too smooth. But I love the smell. And I love the bonfire and the forest. We all find branches and the helpers help us make bows and arrows. Some of the boys play Kill the Romans. The Romans were our Enemy long ago. We always have Enemies it seems.

Baby Diary

January 29, 1956
The girl is developing nicely. She sits up by herself and crawls backwards. I nurse her in the morning and in the evening. She's eating well. Two weeks ago she went on strike and wouldn't eat anything, maybe because of her vaccine.

The girl is quiet, relaxed and very cute. She babbles in a loud voice.

There are now six babies in the Baby House—three and three in the two rooms. She laughs at everyone and is very social. Each day at 11:00 I come and spend half an hour with her.

This month the doctor gave her a general examination. The doctor said she has an unusually fine body with very fine legs. And it's true, she really does hold herself up very well.

Dori

I had a bad dream. Half the children in my Group and maybe also Carmella's Group were standing together on one side and half were on the other side facing them and a huge orange snake was chasing me between the two sides. The children were standing as still as soldiers at attention. As still as statues. I was screaming and running back and forth but the snake wasn't interested in the other children. Only in me. Maybe it didn't even know the other children were alive. Maybe it thought they really were statues. I tried to hide with the other children and stand like a statue too but it didn't work—the snake knew it was me.

Carmella was there too. She was standing nearby and watching with her arms folded and smiling. I was screaming my head off but she didn't do anything.

I woke up but every time I went back to sleep I had that dream again. It went on scaring me like crazy all night long.

Transcript of the Social Committee Meeting May 1967

Chair: Juliette
Present: Shula, Lou, Finkel, Dagan

Juliette: This is a very difficult meeting, so I'll try to be as concise as possible. We have to decide three things, as I see it. First, are we involving the police? Hagar and her parents strongly oppose it and I feel their wishes have to be respected. It's against our policy anyhow, so unless there's any opposition to keeping the police out of it, we can probably get that one over with right away. Anyone opposed?
Shula: No. We all agree.
Juliette: Okay, the next item is that social services can't take Eden until Tuesday. We found relatives he can stay with in Ramat Gan until then. We haven't told them what's going on, for obvious reasons. They can't pick him up, so the question is, do we send him on his own?

Shula: I don't see why not.

Juliette: He might run away.

Dagan: He has ceased to be our problem.

Juliette: Okay, I guess we can deal with that situation if it arises. Who's going to be in charge of getting him to the bus in the morning? He's hiding out in the carpentry shop at the moment, and seems to want to stay there. Also, who's going to bring him food?

Lou: I'll look after it. I guess his kibbutz [stand-in] parents aren't going to say goodbye?

Juliette: They already have. They both went to talk to him last night.

Dagan: The question is, what to do with the entire Group. Eden is not the only problem, as we're all aware.

Juliette: It's an ongoing discussion. I'll ask for it to be on the Meeting agenda again.

Dagan: Do we need someone to burn the entire kibbutz down before we face what's going on in Cactus? Let's admit that integration failed, at least for this Group. No other kibbutz has integration, and now we know why.

Juliette: The other integrated Groups are doing well ... Which brings me to the last question: do we bring a suggestion to the Meeting that from hereon we stop taking children with a delinquent background, we form a selection committee, and we pick and choose those who would fit in and benefit the most?

Dagan: I'm surprised that wasn't the policy all along. If we can only accept a tiny fraction of kids in need anyhow, why not accept those who most deserve a chance? Youth Aliyah has plenty of sweet, motivated, well-adjusted kids who need a place. Why take the hopeless cases they can't find anywhere else to dump?

Juliette: Well, you know Martin's feelings. Everyone deserves a chance, especially those who are most troubled. Where is Martin, by the way?

Dori

We're going to pick mulberries today! We have to put on raggedy clothes because mulberry stains don't come off.

We ride to the trees in a cart. Mummy's Group and my brother David's Group are there too. Everyone climbs the two trees and picks mulberries and eats them. They're incredibly delicious. I'm adding them to my list of favourite foods. Figs and pomegranates and soup almonds and mulberries.

There's an ancient grave near the trees. Yosi Haglili and his son were buried there but it only has bones in it now. Mummy gets very excited every time she talks about that grave. Adults like very old things.

The grave is inside a cave with two gates. Some of the older children dare each other to go inside and the brave ones go past the first gate but no one goes past the second gate. It's too dark.

Finally Mummy says it's time to go back. I'm allowed to go in the cart with the older children because Mummy is their teacher. David comes too. The Group starts singing I'm Just a Lone Wayfaring Stranger in Hebrew. I didn't know it came in Hebrew. We had a record with that song on Davaar Street. I'm going home to see my mother I'm going home no more to roam I'm just a going over Jordan I'm just a going going home. Jordan is an Enemy but in the song it's more like Yehupitz.

I'm Just a Lone Wayfaring Stranger and Gone Are the Days were my two favourite songs on that record. When we went to visit my aunt in Canada everyone always asked me to sing Gone Are the Days

> Gone are the days
> When my heart was young and gay
> Gone are my friends
> From the cot and fields away

182

Gone from this earth
To a better land I know
I hear those gentle voices calling
Old Black Joe

I stood on a chair to sing it. For some reason every-one laughed. I don't know why. It's a sad song—a very sad song. It made me think of Eldar. I was young and gay there and I had friends in the fields and on the cots. I wasn't forced to go to that horrible kindergarten.

After Gone Are the Days I sang We'll Fly Away. When I said the word Fly I jumped off the chair as if I was flying to Neverland. Come to think of it my brother David used to call me Tinkerbell.

Neverland

Dori

Hannah got a present in the mail. It's a doll that stands with a dress made of three layers of sponge—pink and pale yellow and pale green. They're not Pioneer colours and it's not a Pioneer doll. In Eldar we don't have that kind of doll. The kind that's more for decorating than for playing with.

Hannah put the doll on the table next to her bed and she won't let anyone touch it. She put it there to show us that she has it and we don't. She could have kept it in her father's Room.

She keeps saying *this is mine don't touch it.* She wants us to be jealous.

I might bury this doll too.[64]

Thy Neck with Chains of Gold

RICKY   Rita, listen to me … we had a dream, it was my dream and yours. We had enemies inside ourselves, and all around us. So we cast a mold to keep from falling out. But we don't all fit perfectly. So we stretch and pull and weep with pain. But whenever I close my eyes, I see the skeletons of those dry bones, the ones in Ezekiel. That vision of the dry bones rising—the homeless, the wanderers, two thousand years old … they need us to give them life and dignity and flesh.

RITA   I can only think of myself. I have nothing left for them.

RICKY   You have! We'll find our dreams again. We'll build and create like we said we would. If I lost you for a while, it doesn't matter now. I forgive you.

       (ELI *comes running in*)

ELI   It's Michael—he's had an accident on guard duty—

RITA   What are you saying, Eli? Where is he?

ELI   It's okay. Everything will be okay.

Dori

Mummy tells me we'll be leaving Eldar in a few days. We're going back to Canada. We're going by airplane this time. On an airplane when you touch your earlobe it buzzes.

I say *for how long?* and she says *I don't know exactly.*

I hope it's not a long time. I love Eldar.

Diary of a Young Man

20 September 1924. I spent a few weeks away from the commune, travelling through the country. I'd woken one morning and felt that a "bad mood" had come over me. I felt I had to get away for a while and see the rest of the country.

I didn't say anything to anyone, I didn't even inform the roster managers. I knew they'd understand that I left on account of my bad mood; they too experience these things from time to time.

On that day, the number of bad-mood travellers reached eight.

Dori

I'm seven today. I have a birthday party but mostly we run around. It's my first birthday without a dress.[65]

Gilead gives me a white belt folded into a circle. It's patent leather. Now I have something to put in my drawer.

My brother David has a Tin Tin book. I love Tin Tin. David looks at it with me and tells me the story. I don't really understand the story and I can't think of any other story to go with the pictures but I don't care. With colours like these the story isn't important.

Our First Year

13 January 1950. Tremendous preparations now under way for the celebration of Year One at Eldar. Most of us agree that it's been a good year. It didn't go precisely according to plan, we didn't realize everything we wanted, but never mind, there's another year ahead. We look forward to expansion in almost every field. Here are some of the important provisions in the coming year's plan:
- In future years, when we've solved the water problem, we'll try producing fruit here that cannot be grown in any other part of the country. We will continue to tend the hundreds of dunam of olive and fig orchards, plus the 30 or so dunam of workable Arab grapevines.

- Whereas this past year we succeeded in planting only 30 dunam of vegetable crops, in the coming year we will aim for 200 dunam.
- We will put in 300 dunam of silage and pasture.
- We have completed a small but highly satisfactory greenhouse, and we plan to expand our modestly constituted landscaping and vegetable nurseries.
- As compared with last year's planting of 10,000 trees (mainly pine) we expect to plant 20,000 in the coming year.
- The 30 head of cattle will be housed in a brand new barn before the end of the year, and we expect the herd to grow considerably. We will also build a two-storey chicken house to take care of 4,000 laying birds.
- Our twenty-five thousand lira building budget calls for, in addition to the barn and chicken house, a permanent housing unit for members, a children's house, a laundry and a garage.
- We are prepared to do contracting work for the installation of electrical network in neighboring settlements. Our carpentry shop, because of its excellent machinery—including a joiner-planer, shaper-borer and table saw unit, band saw, radial saw, press, plus many handy smaller tools and gadgets picked up in the States—will enable us to do considerable outside work.
- Our shoe repair shop, located in a cozy corner at the rear of the village, now includes sewing machines, a cutter and a skiver, and a burnishing rod, and although we now do all our repair work and turn out home-made sandals, in the coming year we also expect to begin making our own shoes.
- And by no means must we fail to mention that we expect to be receiving a D-8 tractor with bulldozer.

So, in the coming years, we shall keep building. More than anything else, we want new comrades on other high and windy hills in the New-Old land of Israel; and from among all the newcomers who make up this 20th-century Return, we shall greet more warmly than all the rest those who come from our native land, those to whom we dedicate this record of our first year, the pioneers of America.

Dori

Mummy takes me to an office in Akko. It's not as much fun as our last trip. As soon as she's finished she says we have to go back because she has to pack. There's just enough time to buy me a lemon Artik. It drips on everything and Mummy gets into a bad mood cleaning up the mess.

While I was gone everyone learned how to fold their hands so that the finger on top goes in one direction and the finger on the bottom goes in another direction and it looks like one long finger. They won't tell me how to do it because I was away.

I ask my brother David and he shows me the trick. Then we play cat's cradle with string. My brother is very good at cat's cradle.

Then he shows me how it's better when you hold a kaleidoscope up to the light. It really is magnificent how the shapes move and change like snowflakes. David says that no two snowflakes are alike. I wonder how so many shapes can exist because millions of snowflakes have been falling for millions of years.

My brother kisses me and kisses me. He's a good brother.

Alphabetical History of the Conflict in the North District (1948)

abandon abortive accept accessible account accuse actions advance advancing affiliations aged agreed aide-de-camp al-Bi'na al-Malikiya al-Mawasi allow Alma Amir ancestors announce apologised appointed Arab Arab Affairs Committee argued arm armed armoured arms army army-age Arraba assault asses assist astonishment atoned atrocities atrocity attacks attempt attitude attorney general August authorities avoiding Avraham aware away Ayelet B-17s babies back Bar'am barbaric barred Baruch basis Battalion battle Be'eri Bedouin behest believed belongings

187

Ben-Gurion benign Benjamin Bir'im birth bizarrely
blacken blame Bleida bodies body bombing bombs bones
border border-clearing borders born boy bread Brigade
Brigade's brigades broadcasts brother brushfire budge
bureaucratic buried bursts C-47s camp campaign camps
Captain capture captured car Carmel caught causes caves
cease censorial central CGS chains character charged
charges charging chasing child children Christian churches
Circassian circumstances civilians classified clear clerics
climbed clutching collected Colonel columns command
commander committed committees company complaints
concentration conformed confusion conquered conquerors
conquest conquests conscience-stricken constant contained
contingent convents converted conveyed cooperative corps
corpses corresponded costs couched Council countless
country course covered credence criticism crossed
crowded cruel cursorily curtailed Dakotas danger dared
Dawayima deal decided declining defence defended Deir-
Hanna Deir-al-Qasi Deishum deliberately demanded
demanding demented demographic demolished denial
departure depended depopulated depopulation deposited
depositions designated destroy details detention determined
diary died different difficult discovered discretion
discriminating discuss distancing distinction District divide
documentation documents donkeys doubt doubtless down
dozen dress driven dropped drove Druze dug duly
dumped Dunkelman East echelon Eilabun embarrassed
embellished Emmanuel emptied empty encamped
encountered encouraged end ended ends enemy enhance
entry escape escaped establish estimated ethnic
euphemistic everything evicting eviction exaggeration
example except exile exiles exist existence existing exodus
expel expelled expelling explained expressions expulsion
expulsions external eye fact facts failing fall far Farradiya
Fassuta fate father feared fearing felt fielding fight file

Filles de la Charité de la Sacré Coeur find findings fingernails
fire fired flat fled fleeing flight follow-up food force
forced forces Foreign Affairs Ministry fought found four-
year-old framework freeze Friedman friendly front frontier
frustrated future Galilee Galilee's general Gershon Gil'ad
girl goal going Golani gone govern government gradually
grief ground ground-support group grow guard guidelines
guilty gullies Haganah Haifa Haim half-Muslim hand
handful Hanochi hard Harkabi harm's harmed Hashahar
Hayun head headless heard held hills hinterland Hiram
history holding hollow home homes hospitalised hostile
hours houses HQ Hule humane Hurfeish hurt husband
IDF's ignored immigrants implemented impression
improve inaccurate inadequacy indiscriminately infiltration
inhabitants inhabited initial inland input inquiry inside
instinctive instructed instructions Intelligence intensive
intercession interim interior intermittent internal
international investigate investigated investigating
investigation Iqrit Israel Israel's Israeli Isser issued Jann
jeeps Jewish Jews Jishwas job joined June Jurdiye just
Justice Ministry Kafr-Qila Kafr-Manda Kafr-Bir'im Kaukab
keep Khirbet Kibbutz kicked killed killing killings
kilometres kitchen knew knows Komarov lack laid land
lands Laskov last launched leave leaving Lebanese left
legaresh lending Les Dames de Nazareth less letter liaison
Lieutenant life limb limited line liquidated list living
local locals loot looting lost Lt Lubya Maghar main
maintained maintenance Majd-al-Kurum Major majority
males maltreatment man Mano Mansura Maronite
Marriott mass massacre massacres matter means meeting
Meirun members memory men mendacious Mi'ilya
middle might migrated military Minority Affairs Ministry
minorities misdeeds missions mixed moderation months
morale morning Moroccan Moshe mosque mother
motion moved movement mukhtars mules municipality

murder murdered Muslim Muslim–Christian Muslims
Nahum naked names necessity needless negligence
neighbouring nervous never new newly news night Ninth
none non-imperative non-local non-locals northeastward
Northern northwards November nowhere number object
observer observers occupied occupy October Oded
offensive officer officers official sold olive open Operation
operational opinion opposite orchards order ordered
organised original other others outcome Outpost outside
overrun own owners Palestinian Palmah palpably
Panhandle panic parcel part partial partition party passed
passing past path paths patrol pattern patterns peaceful
peasants people perhaps Perlman permanent permission
persisted personnel perspective petty piled Pina planned
pleaded politicians population possessions possibility
POWs preceded precipitate precipitated presumably
prevented prisoners probable probably probe Problem
prohibitions promote property prospect prospective
protected providing punishment Qaddita Qantara Qawuqji
qualified quarters questioned questioning quickly quietly
radio raids Rama Ras-al-Ahmar recalled recommended
recorded records refugee refugees refused rejected religious
religious-ethnic remain remained remaining remnant
removed repeatedly report reprimanded request reserve
resistance resisted respond response responsible rest result
retribution return returned returning revenge Cambridge
right Rihaniya risk Rmaich road roadside robbery rocky
Rosh roughly round rubble rule rumours sadness Safad
Safsaf Sakhnin Saliha Sammu'i Sa'sa Sauda save saw
scattered scope score scouring scraping search secure
Security Segal senior September sergeant served Service
Service\Field settled settlement Seventh severe severely
Shapira Shertok Shimshon shipped Shitrit shock shooting
short shot show sideways sieve silence simply site
situation size sketchy slated slowly smiling soil soldier

soldiers soon sorted south-eastern southward specifically
sped spotted spring squad squadron squads stand start
State stay stayed stiff still stones stopped stranded strict
string strip Studies submit submitted sufficient Suhmata
superfluous support supported surrender surrendered
surrendering surrounding survival survivors sweeps Syrian
systematic Taflas taken taking Tarbikha Tarshiha tea team
Teitaba temporarily tents terms territory tested thinking
throw thrust tilted time tired tons torched training
transfer transferred transmission transport treat tree trek
triggered troops two-week-old UN uncharacteristically
unclear undefinitive underlines undermined unfolded
uniform unimportant uninvestigated unit units unjustified
unpunished up uprooted upshot urge vagaries vanished
veered vent veteran viewed Vilensky village village's
villagers villages visible volunteers Wa'ra wadi wake walk
walking war warning was waves welfare wells west
westward what when whole wholly whose why
widespread wife within without woman women wrangle
wrath wrote Ya'akov Yadin Yalan Yanuh year years
Yehoshafat you

Dori

Mummy wakes me up before anyone else is awake. It's
still dark outside.

I can't decide whether to take the belt Gilead gave me.
I don't really need a belt but if I don't take it Gilead will
think I don't like it. In the end I decide to leave it. It'll be
there for me when I come back.

We go outside to where Daddy is waiting with Sara and
David and the suitcases. It's very quiet on Eldar. Everyone
is still sleeping.

A car comes to take us away. It brings us to a noisy
bus station. It's morning now and there are people

everywhere. Mummy tells David to stay on a bench with me and not move while she goes to clarify something.

There's an old Arab woman sitting beside us on the bench begging. She makes sad sounds. David has some money in his pocket that Mummy gave him. He says *if I could I'd give her all my money.* I say *yes yes give her all the money!* But David shakes his head and says *I can't.* He's right. Mummy gave him the money to take care of.

Then Mummy comes back and we get up and leave.

Balli∂tic Protection∂ Solution∂

Perhaps the most successful kibbutz industry today is Eldar's ballistic protections solutions. Iraq proved to be a gold mine for the factory as U. S. demand for the product increased. The company now employs more than a thousand workers in Israel and 300 in plants abroad. Its turnover has increased from NIS 1.5 billion last year to 3 billion this year.

—*The International Economist,* 2010

Dori

In the evening the plants and bushes have a marvellous smell. The darker it gets the more marvellous the smell gets. The sun is starting to set but it's not dark yet. Soon the Last Rain will fall. We won't know for sure it's the Last Rain until it doesn't rain again. If it doesn't rain again we'll look back and say *that was the Last Rain.*

Notes

1. Optional in Kindergarten; if the Group was small, free play under supervision of the Minder continued until Transitional First Grade.

2. An idea of Utopian communal living, first envisioned by socialist European Jews who settled in Ottoman Palestine in the early 1900s.

3. From Our First Year, a collective diary of Eldar's first year, written in English; no author.

4. The literal meaning of "wig" in Hebrew is "foreign (false) hair" (*pe'ah nokhrit*); the word for "foreign" is also used for "non-Jew." In Modern Hebrew, "non-Jew" is the more common meaning, and the only one Dori has encountered.

5. In 1961, each window served a single Room. Front terraces and curved railings were added in the 1970s; as the kibbutz prospered, walls between individual Rooms were torn down and units were expanded into larger apartments. Below: early stages of construction, 1950.

6. From *Between the Motion and the Act*, an autobiographical novel by Naftali Satie (formerly Stavitsky), written in Montreal during a leave from Eldar. "It was supposed to be a four-month leave and I thought at first I could write the book in six months, but I was working full-time and there were the kids and so on, so in the end I needed a year and a half. I was very happy with Vantage Editions. They did an excellent job—they produced a high-quality book, and they sent out review copies and did promotion just like any other publisher. I had a choice: paperback, which falls apart very quickly, or hardback, which lasts forever. I chose hardback. I had to stay in Canada an extra three months after Varda and the kids went back, to earn the $1,200. Paperback would have taken two months—not much of a difference in the grand scheme of things. At the end of December, Varda went back to the kibbutz and I sublet our place on Davaar Street and moved in with my parents. I took a job as a shipper—it involved a lot of lifting and wrecked my back, but it paid well."

—*Interview with Naftali Satie*

7. Heb. *metapelet* (*f*). Unique kibbutz usage; no equivalent in English; refers to the childcare worker in charge of a Group. The word came to mean, in the 1970s, counselling psychologist/ psychiatrist—see B'Tipul, the award-winning Israeli TV drama adapted by HBO in the USA as *In Treatment*. In general usage, the root verb means "looking after" and, as in English, has a wide range of connotations, from benevolent to sinister. I've always associated the word *metapelet* with refuse drifting on drainage water—orange peels, for example; or with something bloated abandoned in an alleyway; I can't say the word, can hardly bear to hear it spoken or even see it printed, especially in English transliteration, on a page.

8.

In kibbutz usage, "Group" (*kvutzah*) refers to a group of boys and girls, close in age, who live together in a Children's House. Above, Dori's Group in the Baby House; Dori to the far right. Below, a few months later.

9. Modern Hebrew for "hoe"; borrowed from Arabic.

10. Small crouton-like puffs produced by Osem and, as far as I know, unique to Israel; made of flour, oil, and spices. Highly addictive.

11. Hebrew is an inflected language, and five of the six words that entertain Dori and Lulu rhyme: *sinorim nir'im matzḥikim al anashim agulim.*

12. Interview with the curator, from John R. Snarey, "Becoming a kibbutz founder: An ethnographic study of the first all-

American kibbutz in Israel," *Jewish Social Studies* 46:2 (1984:Spring) © Indiana University Press.

13. Possibly this was Shoshana's chance to nibble choice items. She carried meals from the Kitchen to the Children's House on a milkmaid's yoke, three metal containers hanging from either side. We remember the secretiveness and concentration of her turned back at the counter, as she unloaded and distributed the food. In a diary written shortly after my twelfth birthday, I found the following entry: *Shoshana used to go down and come back with food. You had to go down a few steps and walk a great deal from our quarters to the dining room and it must have been pretty hard on Shoshana. But through all her hardships, and probably because of them, she was … —but let us leave that to later.*

14. Written in 1967 by Varda Satie (née Klein); b. 1927, Montreal, Canada. "The main character in the play is single. I was already married on the kibbutz. I met Naftali at the local [Montreal] branch of *Shomer* [Young Guard Youth Movement] when I was fourteen. He was four years older than me and had just volunteered for the army. I had a huge crush on him—he was famous for having Paul Newman eyes, 'bedroom eyes' we used to call it. All the girls had a crush on him. I gathered my courage and asked if I could write to him in the army. He said he'd be flattered to receive letters from such a pretty girl, but we only got to know each other later, on his leaves and through letters. He wrote me over a thousand letters from his base. I know because I numbered them. I don't know where the letters are now; they were lost. He wrote to me just about every day—long, beautiful letters.* It was always a thrill, getting those envelopes in the mail. Naftali was lonely in the army, and bored. He asked to go overseas, but they needed him at Gander [in Newfoundland]. All his friends from *Shomer* were overseas, but the army wouldn't send him. He used to tell me what books to read and what to look for in the books—he was educating me. At first he signed his letters 'with impending love'—he was

always a stickler about language. Then he began leaving out the 'impending' and one day he signed 'your impending husband.' He applied for leave to get married, but soldiers couldn't get leave from Newfoundland very easily, it was too far. He had to wait until the war was over.

"Even then he wasn't released right away, but he was finally given leave in June and we got married. I was seventeen, almost eighteen. I moved in with his parents—I was in teacher's college by then. He returned to the base for a few more months, and when he came back we began preparing to emigrate to Palestine. We didn't sail until 1948—I had to finish my studies and then we had to go to the *Shomer* farm in Highstown, New Jersey, to get *hakhshara* [training]. On the ship to Palestine, or Israel as it was by then, we suddenly heard Arabic on the radio, and all the women began to cry. It hit us how far we were from home. On our first night in Haifa we were given a room with straw mattresses on the floor. Martin found a bottle of whiskey in the port and I got quite high. I stood on the table and sang 'Bei Mir Bist du Schoen.' No one ever forgot that."

—*Interview with Varda Satie*

* *From Nafatli Satie's unpublished memoir fragments:*

In the army I found an enormous amount of free time and to my happy astonishment, well-stocked libraries almost everywhere I was stationed. I first arrived on the mid-Atlantic RCAF station in Newfoundland in late summer 1942. I resumed my prolific correspondence with about a dozen individuals, including my family, Movement friends and, of course, Varda. When I enlisted, my knowledge as journeyman electrician may have saved my life. Try as I might to transfer out to a frontline unit to gain experience that might be useful in Palestine, I was consistently rejected; experienced electricians were in short supply.

One day I received orders to report to the station's legal officer. I entered Captain Solomon's office and, as required, saluted. The fair, balding officer looked up from his desk, smiled sweetly and motioned for me to sit down. His motion as much as said, let's dispense with all these absurd formalities.

"You may be wondering why I asked you here. It's your letters. You probably realize that the officers here come from diverse backgrounds and some of them react very graphically, I mean orally and very publicly, to some of the contents of your letters. In other words, Leading Aircraftsman Stavitsky, you've become quite a celebrity in the officers' mess."

I felt the blood rush to my head. But it was a good feeling. I got them to think, I made them uncomfortable.

"So what's the problem, sir?" I asked.

"Do you mind if give you some advice?" Solomon looked kind and affable.

"Nossir."

"Well, can you cut down on your, er, romantic terms? Yes, your romantic terms and your political views?" There was a hint of regret in his voice.

"Nossir, I cannot. I don't see why I should. This war is being fought for the preservation of democracy and freedom, I thought."

"That's exactly what I mean," Solomon responded quickly. "Those political pronouncements. And Jewish issues. Against the British. It's embarrassing for me and the two other Jewish officers."

"I'm sorry about that, sir, but it's my right and privilege to write what I want."

Solomon suggested I bring my mail directly to him from then on. That system worked until he was transferred. I again deposited my mail in the regular post office. Two weeks passed and I was required to report to Major Susan Musgrove, Commanding Officer of the Women's Division. On her desk lay a letter written in Yiddish.

"What language is that, LAC Stavitsky?"

"Yiddish, ma'am."

"How am I supposed to understand that?"

"I don't know, ma'am."

"Well, you can't write in a language that no one can read."
The deep frown never left her rather handsome middle-
aged face.

"Excuse me, ma'am, but what do you think I write to
my parents that requires censorship?" I experienced a
debilitating sense of frustration.

"I don't care what you write to your parents as long as it's
in English."

"What about French?"

"Don't be snarky, Airman," she shot back in apparent anger.

"My parents can only read Yiddish and I believe it's my
privilege to write to them."

"LAC Stavitsky, this interview is terminated. French or
English."

I went directly, letter in hand, to the Catholic padre. He
was a red-faced jovial-looking man. When he heard the story
his round face crinkled and he laughed. "Bring me your
letters. Promise me that you will not include any military
information. Directly, or in any other way."

The padre subsequently was also transferred and once
again my letters went straight to the post box.

Knowing that the officers were discussing my letters,
the letters became, in part, didactic. I described in detail
to Varda the activities of the Women's Division, the pro-
liferation of pubic lice amongst the airmen. I reported on
anti-Semitism on the base and in the world at large. I criticized the deplorable policies of the British in Palestine and
reviewed the books I had read. In short I had a captive audi-
ence and I did my best to score points.

Some weeks later my name again appeared on the Daily
Routine orders to report to the medical officer.

The doctor was a very short pudgy man with a boxer's
face. His name could have been Jewish, but he was a Toronto

Presbyterian. He politely asked me to sit and relax. I sat and waited. Finally he spoke.

"I censored your letter last night in the officers' mess. I was intrigued by your comment on Arthur Koestler's Arrival and Departure. Can I borrow it?"

I brought him the book and subsequently, at his request, all my mail.

"I won't read your letters, but you must be aware that they arouse some pretty wild reaction in the mess. You will be well-advised to bring me your mail."

It seemed obvious to me that the doctor was lying. Not only did he want to read my letters, he wanted to discuss them. At first I felt inhibited, but then, conversely, I experienced a sort of exhilaration. "He wants excitement, this doctor, I'll damn well give it to him." At one of our meetings, always pleasant—the batman served tea and wonderful pastry—the doctor made a startling statement. "You want a discharge, I can get it for you."

"Why do you think I want a discharge?"

"Because you hate it here."

"But you also know, I'm sure, that I've been requesting transfers to an aircraft carrier, far cry from a discharge."

"From your letters, the message I get is that you want out."

"What kind of discharge do you have in mind?"

"On mental grounds."

"You must be kidding, Doctor. Thanks, but no thanks."

About a month later, I arrived to deliver my mail. This time the batman was absent and the doctor himself ushered me in. He was wearing only underwear. Instead of the batman, the doctor himself served tea, waddling around, his rather sizable posterior appearing to be doing its own separate exercises. The talk, in reference to some book, turned to sex. The doctor asked, "Do you have any 69 experience?"

I stared somewhat blankly at him. I had absolutely no idea what the man was talking about. The doctor, realizing his faux pas, abruptly stood up, cup in hand, and dismissed me. I deposited my next letters in the mailbox.

Weeks later I was again summoned to the doctor. I assumed he would request that I resume bringing my mail to him. However the doctor greeted me in full dress, his brass buttons and bars glistening.

"I've been transferred, and before I leave I wanted to thank you for the pleasure being your friend was for me and here is a little token of my esteem." He handed me a small flat box, neatly wrapped. I thanked him for the gift, and for the time he had spent censoring my letters.

"Perhaps when this is all over you can look me up," the doctor responded. We shook hands.

Back in the barracks I unwrapped the gift and found a very fine leather wallet with the doctor's name engraved in gold.

One more mail incident occurred. This time the order to report was to the Chief Provost, the top man in the Military Police establishment on the station. This was apparently serious business and I was far more apprehensive than on previous occasions.

Outside the office I was immediately treated as a prisoner. The sergeant-at-arms asked me to surrender my hat and belt and marched me into the Provost's office. The Provost had a magazine open on his desk. He dismissed the sergeant and kept me standing at attention in front of his desk. He looked up. "Do you really read this shit?"

I inhaled deeply and relaxed. If this was about reading, no problem.

"I don't know what you're referring to, sir."

"This piece of shit." He lifted the journal so that I could identify its name: Youth Horizons.

"Yes, sir, I do read it."

"Do you agree with what's written?" The Provost glared hatefully.

"Generally I do. Yessir."

"Do you agree with this?" He again held up the magazine to display an article entitled 'The Death of Lord Moyne.'"

"Well, sir, I don't know. I haven't been able to read it yet since you have it here."

"None of your shit now, Airman! I don't know whether I should give this to you." His British accent was getting thicker.

"This is a Zionist magazine, sir. It's against Hitler."

"This Stern gang here, Zionists too, no? And they murdered a British diplomat. In cold blood. Stavitsky, you're dismissed. I can't stand the sight of you. I pity you. Here, take this piece of fuckin' shit."

15. The beautifully produced edition was Italian, with illustrations by Libico Maraja (1912–1983). The text had been translated into Hebrew, but Naftali paraphrased and toned down the story.

16. The reference is to a general assembly (in Hebrew, *siḥa*, the common term for "conversation"). At one time pivotal to the functioning of the commune, these weekly meetings were initially governed by only rudimentary rules of order and had no quorum requirements. The kibbutz Secretary served as chair; when the presiding Secretary's tenure was up, the nomination committee approached members who were considered desirable. Candidates, if there were more than one, were presented at the Meeting and often listed reasons they did not think they'd be suitable; the most reluctant candidates were usually the ones chosen. The system is much more variable today,* but according to Nissim, the one topic everyone still votes on is membership: whom to accept for a trial period, who has passed the trial period, who must leave.

Committees (a kibbutz of four hundred members may have as many as thirty committees) have always handled specific issues as they arose; members who are not happy with the committee's decision, or committees who do not feel they are up to dealing with a given situation, can ask the Secretary to bring the matter to the meeting. In the early days, meetings were frequently stormy, but as the years passed the emphasis moved from ideology to efficiency.

* Sorry it's taken me so long to answer. My role as Secretary means I'm up to my ears in work.

Regarding your question: even on the most privatized kibbutzim there is still a *siḥa* at least three or four times a year because the kibbutz is a collective and there are decisions which for legal reasons must be reached at a members' meeting. The alternative to the *siḥa* is different on different kibbutzim—some have a "council" of 30 members who reach decisions on collective issues; others continue to grant the main committees (Economic and Social Secretariat) the role of acting managers; and yet others allow the people who hold the positions to make decisions on their own.

At our kibbutz we have a *siḥa* about once a month and 30 out of 300 members show up. There is no voting during the *siḥa*, the voting is by a ballot box which is placed in the Dining Hall on the Friday and the Sunday after the meeting. At Galron, for example, the issues are divided into the type that are voted on during the meeting by a show of hands; those that take place during the meeting but by a ballot box in the Dining Hall; and those that are voted on by open ballot in the days following the meeting. In short, the kibbutzim are struggling with direct democracy.

All the best,

Rakefet

17. In biblical poetry, the inflected *dodi* means "my beloved" (see Song of Songs, 2:8). In general use, however, *dod* is "uncle" and *dodi* is "my uncle." Naftali's use of *doda* ("aunt" in ordinary usage, but borrowed here from the poem) as a pet-name is idiosyncratic. I did find a blog, however, in which an Israeli woman recalled that *doda* was a common pet-name among her fellow conscripts when she was in training.

18. Interview with a founder, from Snarey (1982–1983), "The Social and Moral Development of Kibbutz Founders and Sabras: A Longitudinal and Cross-sectional Cross-cultural Study," Doctoral dissertation, Harvard University, Cambridge, MA (Gutmann Library No. Sn19; Pusey Library No. HU90.11684.50), 224.

19. The Hebrew word for gizzards is *kurkevan*, but in colloquial Modern Hebrew the word is more commonly used to refer to bellybuttons. Because of this linguistic overlap, Dori thinks the cooked gizzards from the Kitchen are bovine navels. This may be a widespread misconception among Israeli children, especially since the Modern Hebrew slang for "bellybutton," *pupik* (from Yiddish), is also used to refer to the dish.

20. Eldar members took turns patrolling the border of the settlement; all were trained to use a rifle, though the ability to aim of many members was uncertain. The Night Guard was a second guard who was stationed at the Infants' House and who checked on the Children's Houses at regular intervals. Night Guards at Eldar were equipped with a walkie-talkie connected to loudspeakers inside the Houses. At times, if a baby was sick or a parent insisted, the roster manager assigned Night Guard duty to the parent concerned, but as a rule, assignations were arranged in accordance with kibbutz principles.

21. **Novelist55:** Did anyone on yr kibbutz call their parents by their first names?

    Nissim73: No.

    Novelist55: My brother told me they tried in the beginning to get the kids to use first names, at least on Shomer kibbutzim. But the kids switched to abba [father/dad] and ima [mother/mom] as soon as they understood what the words meant. So the parents stopped trying. In my brother's group everyone switched except him. He only switched once he got to Canada.

    Nissim73: Do you have an eBay account by any chance?

22. The line was changed for the sake of rhyme; a literal rendition would read: "We struck him/And he began to cry." This once-popular street song was sung to the tune of the "Mexican Hat Dance." Contributors to internet chat rooms recall several versions; in some it is "Moishe" or "Yankele" who either gets hit or eats ice cream/an egg/an omelette. In other versions, after "Abdallah" receives the blows, he is taken to a National Health Clinic, where his underpants are removed. Eldar children would have picked up the racist version from visiting children, Combat Pioneer soldiers posted at Eldar, Israeli volunteers, and/or resident city children.

23. "Hallah" is a biblical word (see Ezekiel 43:27), meaning "onwards" or "further"; it may originate from the interjection HA-LA-AH. In Arabic, the highly idiomatic Yallah, which probably evolved from Ya-Allah (O God), has by coincidence (?) a similar meaning: "let's go," "get a move on," "hurry up." Modern Hebrew has adopted the Arabic idiom and expanded its usage.

24. *Tiger, Tiger Burning Bright* by Paul Burlin (1886–1969).

25. *Landscape with Garage Lights* by Stuart Davis (1894–1964).

26. *Guerrillas* by Joseph Hirsch (1910–1981).

27.

והוא יִהְיֶה לְרוּחִי חָתָן.

28. Dori is unfamiliar with the Hebrew for "prophet" (*ha-navi*) and confuses it with the word for "grapes" (*anavim*).

29. In 1961 an unusually cold and rainy winter led to shortages of vegetable crops.

30. In Modern Hebrew, the word *zona* is equivalent to "whore" (in biblical Hebrew the word is closer in nuance to "harlot"). According to Hebrew's usual gender markers, the masculine of *zona* would be *zoneh*; the masculine form, however, does not exist.

31. Camp Bilu'im, a Young Judea camp for older teenagers, was named after the small Zionist movement BILU (a Hebrew acronym based on Isaiah 2:5—*House of Jacob, let us go*) which was founded in Russia in 1882 in response to a wave of pogroms. In colloquial Modern Hebrew *bilu'im* refers to enjoyable activities (derived from Job 21:13). The homonymic overlap is coincidental.

32. Dori's account is translated from Hebrew. Since Hebrew has fewer words than English, one term often serves many purposes, and words which seem advanced for a young child (*unfortunately, symbol, longing*) are everyday words in Hebrew. When Dori switches to English, the text is printed in an alternative font.

33. For the banned rendition, see www.youtube.com/watch?v=d43h6tJlgUY.

34. *Dimitri, just back from reserve duty, recalls:*
    I first heard about Petra when the army sent me to guard an archaeological expedition, but I didn't think of going

there until I heard about Meir's trip. We considered Meir a demigod, we followed his every thought; if Meir could go, why couldn't we?

The trip to Petra was only one of the plans floating around back then. For example, there was a plan to go to Mecca. They wanted me to join, but it was cancelled for a thousand reasons. We decided to go to Petra. We wanted to know what people are like there. Nabataean sand. Castles. It aroused our curiosity. And also the danger, to prove something about ourselves—the fighters of the 890 [Paratroopers Brigade]. Our military service wasn't dangerous enough, it wasn't life-threatening.

I met Dror, may he rest in peace, in the army. He was a guy with ambition. A good friend. Loyal. One of those healthy, well-built types, walked tall. Back then there were no jeeps. Patrols went out on foot for days, weeks, months. One day we were patrolling in the Judean desert, in the evening, and we sat next to the Cave of Horror [where Jews are believed to have taken refuge in the war against the Romans in 133–135 CE], we lit a bonfire, drank coffee, and Meir told us about Petra.

Later, when Dror and I were patrolling together in Jenin, we began to talk about the Red Rock again. On the way back we had to submit a report to the Northern Command. As it happened, there was a 1:1000-scale map lying around. Dror and I nicked it, and we began planning our trip.

I don't remember exactly when we left, but it was around Passover 1956. I didn't know who had gone before us, but I did know we were following in the tracks of a man and a woman.

We went out at dusk and walked all night. We came across a Bedouin tent and we bypassed it. In the morning we got to Petra. When we saw it, our eyes widened. We'd heard about it but we never imagined this.

We continued as far as we could, walking a few dozen metres behind a group of hikers. A guide was telling them about the history of the city in English. I don't speak English but Dror understood. We took what photos we could and saw what we could. We didn't get too close; in any case, we were in uniform. Uniform and Australian hats. I had the camera. The pictures didn't come out that well, we weren't great photographers. Today the photos are all over the place—Davidi [Gen. Aharon Davidi, then Paratrooper Commander] has some, and Arik [Ariel] Sharon, and other people.

We walked until 3:00 in the afternoon and then we headed back. When we got to the mountain of Ras al Naqab, we saw an eight-man patrol approaching. They were about fifty metres away and didn't notice us.

We hid near a ditch. When they reached the path, they saw that the footprints in the sand suddenly vanished. They began to look for us and when they found us they opened fire from both sides. We killed two of them and even took loot— a small knife, an English rifle, binoculars and other things.

We had an Uzi and a Czech rifle. When they began shooting, we had to return fire. I fired first and Dror covered me. I was wounded in my hand and leg. Then I covered Dror, and he was shot in the head and died on the spot. I went over to him, took his compass, the maps, and the Uzi. Bullets were flying all around me, they hit my canteen, my grenade carrier, my hat. I tried to run. I ran along the path. I felt the blood dripping; I saw blood stains. I bandaged the wound on my hand.

Next to the path there was a ravine. I had no choice. I jumped four metres and sprained my ankle. I hid in the ravine. I had to wait for hours, until dark. They continued to look for me until nightfall.

At night I climbed out and headed back towards Petra. I skirted it and returned not by the path that we came on but through Wadi Musa [lit. Valley of Moses, then a tiny village, today a small tourist town].

I walked slowly, leaning on the barrel of the rifle. All night I walked. On the patrol path I came across a smuggler on a camel. He shot at me and I shot at him. I only wanted to take his camel and ride it back but I missed him.

Before we left, we'd arranged with friends that they would wait for us near the memorial. The signal was three shots on either side. I saw them in the distance. They were sitting on the memorial. I didn't know whether they would recognize me. I was wearing an undershirt on my head. We'd been two and I was now alone. I fired three shots and they responded. Suddenly I realized I didn't have any bullets left. But they saw through their binoculars that it was me and they sent two people to help me.

They bandaged me, gave me water, and sent me to the hospital. On the radio it was announced that two had died on the way to Petra, then things were clarified. When I got better, I had to stand trial, but I was acquitted. In return I had to complete an officers' training course. That was an order from Arik Sharon—he would try to get me off and in exchange I had to take a course.

The trial was a long story. Meir Har Tziyon came to testify and Aharon Davidi and Arik Sharon. They testified on my behalf, saying that patrols often go to distant areas. After that Dror's parents sued me, how come he was killed and not me, how come I was acquitted. But I wasn't found guilty in the civil suit either.

A few months after this, when others were killed going to Petra, it wasn't because of anything I said. I didn't give anyone directions or anything like that.

But after they were killed I was discharged from the army. They simply sent me home.

I feel at one with myself regarding my trip to Petra. Though of course it does weigh a little on my conscience. But it was Dror's idea too. It was equal, both of us. I didn't force him to go, he went of his own free will. But all the same it weighed on me quite a lot. And I was kicked out of the army.

—Interview for *Ma'ariv*, 1971

35. The fifty-page dual-language Haggada was typed painstakingly over a period of several weeks and printed on a mimeograph machine. A neighbouring kibbutz helped with the Hebrew typing and translation. From the Haggada:

> *How is this night different from all other nights?*
>
> *That on this night we, Jewish youth from America, celebrate Passover in Eldar in the Galilee.*
>
> *That we have the night* [Hebrew version: right] *to celebrate our holiday in a conquered Arab village?* [Hebrew: no question mark]
> *That we prophesy about our future.*
>
> *Why are we celebrating our holiday in an Arab village?*
> *One year ago, the fields we tend today were tended by others. And when we came, the desolation of their lives cried out to us through the ruins they left behind. Cried to us and reached our hearts, coloured our everyday lives. One day they were here and the next they were gone. Victims of war. So we search for justification for the right to be here.*
>
> *It isn't difficult to imagine how life must have been. Here a slipper, there a mirror, here a sack of grain, there a family portrait, a broken toy, a student's English textbook.*
>
> *Daily I walk the familiar paths*
> *With open eyes that see not*
> *Not only bitter but rank*
> *Is our once-hallowed ground*
> *And blood too stains our hands*
>
> *Who said "might is right"*
> *And "our cause is just"?*
> *Babies' shoes need no explaining*
> *A civilization gone in one blow*
> *To dream perhaps will heal the wounds*
> *And so with shame seeing nought*
> *We go on building.*

*What gives us the right to reap the fruit of trees we have not
planted? On what moral grounds shall we stand when we take
ourselves to court?*

*Because we have taken upon ourselves the task of Pioneers
and because Pioneering is more than the romantic notion of
coming to a clean, untouched land and planting one's own
clean, fresh seeds. Because building a homeland requires more
than physical sacrifice, dirty hands and a bent back—it requires
a spiritual struggle and a spiritual sacrifice. Because we must
learn to translate our final ideology into the reality of a nation's
fight for existence, and if that reality should require the accomplishments of tasks which are painful to us, all the more will it
strengthen us. And only we can camp on the borders.*

*Because once a Jewish community stood here and a Jewish
community will again arise. (Indeed can it be said that Eldar
itself belongs to any one nation throughout the ages of men's
existence?) For those who died in the concentration camps
and the battles bequeath to us our life here.*

*Let the nation remember those who were cut down in Exile
and did not live to see the glory of Israel—*

*Let the nation remember the brave sons who fell among the
ghetto walls—*

*Let the nation remember the sons and daughters who died
on the cruel waves and thorny roads on the way to their
homeland—*

*Let the nation remember the best of its children, strong of
heart and pure of vision, who bore arms in defence of the life
of Israel, its independence and its freedom.*

36. In the 1967 diary I recount a small sequel to these events:

*In the middle of my nap, I heard someone walking around. I
opened my eyes and sat up in bed.*

Elan, I said. Shoshana untied you?

Oh yes, he answered, a long time ago.

Probably a guilty conscience.

37. From the memoirs of Yehuda Polani, quoted in Yuval Dror, *The History of Kibbutz Education.*

38. The image originated in an illustration of mythological figures in Ancient Greece.

39. This would be the Chubby Checkers version, currently available on YouTube.

40. The Hebrew for "horse" is *sus.*

41. Hebrew for cyclamen.

42. *Anokhi* is a biblical term for the first person pronoun "I"; it is obsolete in Modern Hebrew, other than in poetry. For the painting Dori associates with Anokhi see *The Wanderer* by George Grosz (1893–1959). The original hangs at the University of Rochester Memorial Art Gallery.

43. **Novelist55:** I read that girls automatically and universally demand separate showers when they're 12.

  Nissim73: Yes, I think that's right.

  Novelist55: But in the documentary, one woman remembered that she already wore a bra and had her period etc. in grade 5 but she had to shower with the guys until the end of grade 6 and she was very embarrassed.

  Nissim73: I think that's what the film wants to show—the group and the collective were more important than the individual.

  Novelist55: What about in your group, with the 2 girls?

  Nissim73: 3 girls

  Novelist55: oh right 3

  Nissim73: In our case the girls were younger than most of the boys so that it was actually the boys who didn't want to shower with the girls. You know he mostly interviewed people who left the kibbutz long ago—people who are still on kibbutz really really don't like this film. They feel it's distorted.

Novelist55: Well he does leave out one part. We were encouraged to think independently. I don't know about the other kibbutz movements but I think that's true of all the Shomer kibbutzim no?

Nissim73: Yes but at the same time you were being guided in a certain direction. It was partly insidious.

Novelist55: Did you see city people as inferior?

Nissim73: I guess if I thought about it, but it wasn't on my mind.

Novelist55: Where did Ran Tal get all that incredible footage?

Nissim73: He did amazing archival work. I'm dog-sitting by the way and there's no Internet here, I'm using the neighbour's. It's a weak connection, so I might get cut off any minute.

44. October 5, 1973: Shoshana, whom I've asked to see, sits on a deck chair outside her Room, dressed entirely in black. She appears to be at ease; she's taking time off, enjoying the afternoon sun. I say hello and introduce myself. Shoshana shades her eyes and says, "I remember you. You had a good trick for getting rid of hiccups. Block your ears with both hands and drink a glass of water in one go. It worked."

45. In order to boost the thinning population of Eldar, the Young Guard Federation encouraged a group of young Israel-born adults to join Eldar in 1954. Most were recruited from the Young Guard Youth Movement. A second group followed four years later. In both cases, most of the new arrivals did not last, and by 1960, only 14 percent of the Israel-born members remained. In 1961 the population hovered at 102 adults, 59 kibbutz-born children, and 42 city-born children; a year later it was down to 60 adults. (See Snarey, 1984)

"Every time we sat down for a meal in the Dining Hall, if he was sitting at that table he'd get up and move to another table. He was a heartless man."

—*Interview with Naftali Satie*

46. Mess or chaotic situation.

47. *The Songs We Sing*, illustrated by Hendrik Willem van Loon (1882–1944). The book was a gift for Varda from Dafna, later Lulu's mother, and the handwritten inscription reads:

> *12/2/47*
> *Dear Chavera* [comrade]—
> *It has been a real joy to me—your finding the Tongue to the magnificent language of music—keep using it—add to your vocabulary daily—turn and twist your new-found idioms until they become your own—*
>
> *Wait for me—and together we will speak—in the voice of the world—*
>
> *Dafna*

48. Inn or pub.

49. From Yuval Dror, *The History of Kibbutz Education*.

50. From the 1922–1944 diary of a young man known only as Takḥi, member of a Young Guard commune engaged in paving a road in lower Haifa and then in swamp drainage and stone clearing; the commune later founded Kibbutz Mishmar Ha'emek.

51. DDT.

52. The Hebrew for "storm" is *sa'ara*.

53. "The Brave One"; the film won a 1957 Academy Award for best story, though the writer, Dalton Trumbo (of *Johnny Got His Gun* fame), was blacklisted at the time on suspicion of communist affiliation and could not claim it.

54. Pansies

55. **Novelist55:** Were you afraid of the dark?

    Nissim73: What do you mean "were"?

    Novelist55: Yes, I remember you like to sleep with the light on.

    Nissim73: When are you coming again? You haven't seen my new place in Jaffa.

    Novelist55: I don't know.

    Nissim73: What time is it there?

    Novelist55: Seven. We haven't turned the clock back yet.

    Nissim73: I went swimming last night in the sea. It was past midnight, there was hardly anyone there, it was so beautiful, the waves rolling in. I missed you.

    Novelist55: I wouldn't have been able to go in with you anyhow.

    Nissim73: Oh yes, I remember, you get a rash.

    Novelist55: Were you at the demo yesterday?

    Nissim73: You mean against the oath? No, I didn't feel like it. Too tired after work.

    Novelist55: How was work?

    Nissim73: Next you'll ask me about the weather. How's the book going?

    Novelist55: I'm almost finished. I have this sense, but it could be wrong ...

    Nissim73: ?

    Novelist55: Remember Sweet Mud?

    Nissim73: The film?

    Novelist55: Yes. Remember the Minder from hell?

    Nissim73: yes

    Novelist55: She washes their mouths with soap. And she gives this lecture on sex ...

    Nissim73: yes

    Novelist55: I could tell it wasn't a Shomer [Young Guard] kibbutz.

    Nissim73: Because of the sex?

Novelist55: Because of the authoritarianism. I mean it's all connected. You need that totally progressive radical approach that Shomer had to counteract the dangers of the collective ...

Nissim73: I don't know about that. I always felt the adults were trying to emasculate us. This concept they had back then, teaching us to obey and also suffer a little along the way.

Novelist55: So you don't think it's related to being Shomer or not ...

Nissim73: I don't know. Sometimes I visit another kibbutz, it's like walking into a movie set, it feels so unreal. Even if you go to the same place ten years later, it's already a whole new story.

Novelist55: Just like no two families ...

Nissim73: Except the happy ones, which don't exist.

Novelist55: Still, Shomer had very progressive ideas about kids, education, etc.

Nissim73: Didn't you say Shoshana tied kids to the bed?

Novelist55: One kid. But she did it secretly. If they'd known, they would have been shocked. They still don't know. One guy from Eldar wondered about something I said in an interview and he asked me what I was referring to. When I told him about Shoshana, he wrote back *Everyone here remembers Shoshana as a warm, caring person.*

Nissim73: So what else is new ...

Novelist55: But in Dror Shaul's film everyone accepts that Minder. Her policies are the policies of the kibbutz.

Nissim73: Maybe.

Novelist55: Did you ever get hit?

Nissim73: Yes and no.

Novelist55: ?

Nissim73: We did have one Minder—a guy, actually. He hit us all the time but he disguised it as play. And the problem was that we liked him. And we didn't know how to think about his hitting. I still see him sometimes, at demos. Anyhow, he left the kibbutz.

Novelist55: There was someone at Eldar who did shmirat leila [Night Guarding] who choked and slapped babies. I mean, not everyone likes babies, not everyone is nice or sane. You're in your twenties, you're exhausted, the babies wake you up for the sixth time, they're not your kids, four of them are shrieking at the same time—not everyone is going to deal with that situation the way they should.

Nissim73: How do you know?

Novelist55: Everyone knows when things happen to them. What I can't know is whether it was only the once or more than once. And I'll never know who. Why does that surprise anyone?

Nissim73: It's very disturbing.

Novelist55: Well, you don't leave babies with random strangers, it's asking for trouble. Poor Edna, she put so much into bringing us up and then in one night someone undoes it all ... Anyhow we all survived. It's very moving, in Children of the Sun, how one woman says at the end that when she visits her old kibbutz her feet enjoy stepping on the ground—na'im li baragla'im lidrokh. I love that phrase.

Nissim73: What are you wearing?

Novelist55: I always felt lucky that we grew up without inhibitions.

Nissim73:	That may be just you.
Novelist55:	I guess I bought it all. I still don't own any clothes.
Nissim73:	?
Novelist55:	I mean that I only have 5 or 6 items of clothing. I like seeing beautiful clothes on other people but feel strange wearing anything but jeans myself.
Nissim73:	That's definitely just you.
Novelist55:	You mean I can't blame everything on Eldar?
Nissim73:	My parents are into having every latest gadget.
Novelist55:	You mean the whole ascetic ethic is gone ...
Nissim73:	hold on a sec
Nissim73:	ok I'm back, had to check something.
Novelist55:	Rakefet's novel made me realize something. Taboos are there for a reason. They protect the vulnerable.
Nissim73:	What happened on her kibbutz, the pedophile—that can happen anywhere. And people can ignore it anywhere.
Novelist55:	That's true. Did you have a chance to ask your aunt if she knows who that sleepy teacher was, with the honey-coloured hair? I really liked her. I think the early mornings were hard on her ...
Nissim73:	I keep forgetting. I don't talk to her that often.
Novelist55:	I'm trying to figure out how much I want to say about Martin's suicide/accident.
Nissim73:	What happened exactly?
Novelist55:	He was on guard duty, alone for some reason, and he either shot himself or his Sten went off by mistake, which apparently does happen.
Nissim73:	Yes, it happened to someone on our base. Not a Sten of course.
Novelist55:	Poor guy.
Nissim73:	Who, Martin or the guy on my base?

Novelist55: !

Nissim73: Have you ever considered suicide?

Novelist55: No. Life always interested me too much. And especially since I've had my daughter, there's nothing I want more than to look after her. It makes me happy

Novelist55: just to buy her a new toothbrush ...

Nissim73: Do you breathe down her neck?

Novelist55: I'm way too busy, Nissim. What about you? You're not planning to kill yourself I hope.

Nissim73: Are you kidding? And miss the next elections?

Novelist55: :)

Nissim73: You know about the murder-suicide at Ramat Hakovesh? I think it was last year.

Novelist55: Is that a kibbutz?

Nissim73: Yes. I once went out with someone from there. Anyhow, one old guy killed the manager and then himself in an argument over money. Not exactly money, but the whole privatization process.

Novelist55: ?

Nissim73: A lot of kibbutzim are calling in outsiders to manage the process and suddenly after being in charge of your life for forty years and not having to think about money, some stranger is deciding what your job is worth, what your pension should be.

Nissim73: So there's huge resentment and conflict. The transition is too radical. I can really understand that guy. It's cruel, the way it's being done in some places. A blogger said it's straight out of Orwell. I agree.

Novelist55: I keep finding out more and more. And I want to include everything in my novel ... I haven't even dealt with the whole communal sleeping thing. How it started, how it ended. I wanted to include what my father said—that the best thing about Eldar was having my mother to himself in the evenings, without the kids around. But I don't know where to put that.

Nissim73: Don't get overwhelmed.

Novelist55: It's the reason I could never write science fiction. I'd have to figure out a way not to spend the entire novel explaining.

Nissim73: I like that. Kibbutz as scifi.

Novelist55: You know that guy who sued his kibbutz for traumatizing him?

Nissim73: That's sort of a cliché by now, don't you think? I know that guy by the way.

Novelist55: It's a cliché in Israel. But not in the rest of the world.

Novelist55: Besides, I hate that trivializing. It's very Israeli—I mean not only Israeli but it's something you see a lot in Israel. Everyone always saying azov [let it rest] and shtuyot [nonsense]. Especially shtuyot.

Nissim73: You're sentimental.

Novelist55: That's it—it's supposedly the fear of being sentimental but it's really just the ordinary fear of feeling.

Nissim73: Well if we felt everything here, the streets would empty out, we'd all be locked up in psychiatric wards. Apart from Baruch Marzel, he's indestructible.

Novelist55: Trauma as a way of life?

Nissim73: Exactly. I don't mean victim trauma. I mean watching the country fall apart trauma. Listen, don't worry about including everything.

Novelist55: It's not that I'm worried. It's that I have so much I want to say but at the same time I like

	to be spare. I like to leave rabbit holes for the reader to fall into. By the way, thanks for picking up the permission slip from Maariv.
Nissim73:	You're welcome.
Novelist55:	You know one book club I went to, there was this Jewish woman there, around my age or a bit older
Novelist55:	and she was so upset that in my first novel there are negative references to the kibbutz.
Novelist55:	I mean, she really has this vision, even though it goes against all logic and reason, of the barefoot soldier dancing in the sand with her braid flying
Novelist55:	of a perfect place with perfect people
Novelist55:	a kind of paradise, or even if people aren't perfect, they're all noble and moral and one must think well of them
Novelist55:	even though life must have taught her that humans are the same everywhere, that the entire species is fucked up. But not on Eldar ...
Nissim73:	I think you still believe that yourself. You're still a Zionist.
Novelist55:	Well even Chomsky is a Zionist if you define the word properly. To quote him.
Nissim73:	Here's what I think
Nissim73:	politically, Jabotinsky won
Nissim73:	politically, Jabotinsky was a pacifist next to today's lot. But
Nissim73:	on the non-political level that whole dichotomy, left and right, it's not relevant.
Novelist55:	It is relevant. It's everything.
Nissim73:	Listen
Novelist55:	yes
Nissim73:	You don't want to tell me what you're wearing?
Nissim73:	apart from your jeans, that is ...

Novelist55:	I meant to ask you, can I include our conversations in my novel?
Nissim73:	If you want.
Novelist55:	Do you know the book Nissim and Niflaot?
Nissim73:	no.
Novelist55:	How is that possible? Lea Goldberg ... about a boy and his monkey. The boy is called Nissim and the monkey is called Niflaot. Miracles and Wonders.
Nissim73:	Right now the miracle I'm waiting for is for my air-conditioning to start working again. Guess I'll go to sleep, I've had a long day.
Novelist55:	Don't forget to keep the light on.
Nissim73:	If the world ends, at least I'll be able to see it.
Novelist55:	leila tov matok
Nissim73:	leila tov metuka

56. Literally, a piece of something; commonly used in Modern Hebrew to refer to the segment of a citrus fruit.

57. *Tarzan and the Amazons*, with Johnny Weissmuller (1945); available on YouTube. For the sweeping boy, see part one at 3 minutes, 20 seconds.

58. Credentials were easy to fabricate in the early days of the State, especially in professions where genuine qualifications were in short supply.

59. Snarey, 1982/83.

60. The Hebrew *zefet* means "tar" or "pitch" (see Exodus 2:3—
"And when she could no longer hide him, she took an ark
of bulrushes and covered it with wet earth and pitch"). The
Arabic cognate is *zift* and means both "tar" and "trash"; the
latter is used as an interjection expressing cursory dismissal or
disapproval. Modern Hebrew borrowed both senses of *zift* but
also retained the Hebrew *zefet*, hence Dori's confusion.

61.

A Herd of 120 Goats Was Returned
Yesterday to Lebanon

The goats were led by two shepherds from
Lebanon who entered Israel a few days ago,
north-west of Eldar. Border Guards came
across the shepherds and the goats and took
the goats into custody. The shepherds succeeded in fleeing.

—*Davar*, 7 April, 1960

Lebanese Shepherd Arrested,
His Friend Manages to Escape

Border Guards arrested yesterday at 10:00
A.M. a shepherd from Lebanon near Kibbutz
Eldar when he crossed the border into Israel
with his friend and shepherded his goats.
The two came across the patrolling Border
Guard who ordered them to stop. They did
not obey and began to run towards Lebanon.
One managed to return to Lebanon with the
goats but his friend, age 16, was arrested 400
metres from the border.

—*Davar*, 27 November, 1960

62. In 1951, anthropologists Melford and Audrey Spiro spent a
year observing children at Beit Alpha, the oldest Young Guard
kibbutz (founded 1922). Members of the kibbutz they studied
were reportedly shocked and dismayed when the book based
on these observations came out.

Melford, who by his own account had been warmly wel-
comed during his stay, was now accused of distortion, exaggeration, errors, and incomprehension. Members were stunned
when Melford reported that, between the ages of one and five,

more than half of all observed interaction between the children consisted of acts of physical aggression e.g. hitting, slamming others with an object, kicking, biting, jostling, jumping on, throwing objects at, scratching with fingernails, pulling hair, destroying a toy or game another child was playing with, smearing with food, choking, threatening to cut with a knife, eye-gouging, hair-cutting and penis-pulling.

Melford himself claimed to be the constant target of what he felt was unprovoked aggression, and though he was aware that his work would be compromised if he departed from the observer's stance, he and Audrey sometimes had to intervene, he said, to save a child from being seriously injured when the Minder left the room and asked one of them to keep an eye on things.

No one could explain Melford's "ludicrous" comment that in the past children were not prevented from playing with their faeces; members felt he had misunderstood what he was being told, given the fact that virtually all kibbutzim are obsessed with cleanliness and health.

Most wounding, however, were descriptions of the neglect of infants, whom Melford said could not be cared for properly by one worker, even with the best of intentions.

—Selina R. Korenberg, *Under a Microscope: The Kibbutz as a Subject of Study* (Unpublished Doctoral Thesis)

"At least the Melfords understood basic Hebrew, unlike Bruno [Bettelheim], who didn't speak a word of Hebrew and only spent a few weeks on the kibbutz, mostly writing in his room and asking for favours. He never looked in on the children for more than a few minutes at a time."

—Rafael Avidor, Kibbutz Ramat Yohanan

63. I tried to send you this letter yesterday but I was having trouble with the computer. I think it's working now. I'll do my best to answer your questions, if I can.

—I asked my friends in Canada to send me magazines with pictures so the kids in my class could make collages and posters. We did art, theatre, games—for every topic I taught, I invented a game.

—We made up our own rules regarding babies. Edna was fantastic. We once had a so-called expert from the Federation visit us. I remember Edna was so nervous she broke two bottles. The expert rearranged all the clothes and furniture in the Infants' House and told us we spoil our babies. She felt we picked them up too much and held them too much, and she suggested that Edna should go and observe the European kibbutzim for a month. She also said Spock exaggerated the importance of milk in children's diet. After she left we put all the clothes back in place, picked up the babies, and prepared the milk bottles. Edna was so exhausted she fell asleep in her chair.

—All the outside children had a situation. One came from the Holocaust as a baby with his mother, then the father left. Another boy, the father died and the mother was sick, he was very sweet.

—We had one gay man and one lesbian. Both were very open about it and it wasn't an issue. But they left because they couldn't find partners at Eldar.

—Yes, Tzvi Lipkin had a PhD in nuclear physics. The government took him out of Eldar in 1952, they needed him. I think he was one of the only people in Israel with that background. We see him often when we visit Israel, he's a wonderful person, his wife too. Witty, kind, soft-spoken. I think your politics are the same.

—Yes, we had one evil person on Eldar that I know of and today I wouldn't let him near my baby with a ten foot pole but we were young and trusting. Most of the best people I've known in my life are from Eldar, whether they left or stayed.

I think that covers it. I just came across some anecdotes I wrote down at the time, I think for a magazine. *Dori is one year old. Last week, the mother of a baby in her group took him to visit an aunt in the city. Dori continually patted his bed, sought out his favourite toy, and seemed to look for him in every corner. Upon his return, she literally jumped for joy. She hugged the little boy and tried to say, "I'm so glad you're home."*

I also wrote down your first four words: this, thank-you, abba [daddy], eema [mummy].

Have to run, our friends are at the door, we're going out to eat and see a performance.

Eema

64. In the diary I kept when I was twelve, I recall Hannah's stay at Eldar:

There were seven of us—four boys and three girls—before Hannah came and she wasn't with us very long anyway so I suppose that Shoshana, who looked after us, remembers us as seven. If she remembers us at all, which I really doubt.

I wonder now whether Hannah was really sad to leave us or whether she was overjoyed. Probably the latter; we gave her a most miserable time. Her parents were from Poland and when they came to Israel her father, a dentist, was sent to our Kibbutz for a short while to be our dentist.

Hannah was a very tall and very thin girl, with long yellow hair that was cut short after she came and small blue eyes.

When she first drew a picture was when we started admiring her. On a large sheet of paper, she drew a thin green line at the bottom and the same in blue at the top. Then she drew a few tiny flowers, hardly visible, and one little tree, and filled the rest of the space with light blue. It was very bare, but we all looked up to it. I remember it distinctly because for the whole week when it was hanging up I stared at it, trying in vain to copy her.

But it was no use. My flowers came out big and sloppy and my tree smudged. So after a while I gave up.

But it still remained the thing we looked up to—that is until she mentioned God. Then everything was lost—like a very high building a child makes out of blocks and you put the last block on top—and flop! the whole thing comes crashing down.

I don't remember how it started—maybe someone said my picture is ruined or I didn't sleep well and she answered God has punished you. Then maybe the person burst out laughing and left her wondering what she had said that was so funny. But soon she learned that she was facing a whole lot of children—a whole kibbutz for that matter—that would laugh at her when she mentioned God. And when we teased her she always cried God will punish you—God will punish you.

She left soon after that.

65.

Above, the only photo of that event. Varda and Naftali were already under a cloud, having informed the kibbutz of their decision to leave for good. Only their closest friends bade them goodbye.

Acknowledgments

I am grateful to the many people who allowed me to weave real-life fragments into the fictional loop:

Excerpts from *Our First Year* are from *The Launching: Sasa's First Year* (1951), in theory written collectively but mostly, it seems, the work of one member. Some names and a few dates have been changed. Many thanks to Keren Hayesod–United Israel Appeal for allowing me to resurrect this archival document.

Excerpts from *Between the Motion and the Act* are from an autobiographical novel written by my late father, Nahum Ravel. The novel was translated into Hebrew and published under the title *Second Thoughts;* it was the sequel to an earlier work, *Falls the Shadow,* which my father wrote during his leave from Kibbutz Sasa (1959–1961). *Falls the Shadow* was handsomely produced by Vantage Editions.

The *Baby Diary* passages were written in touching, second-language Hebrew by my mother, Aviva Ravel, when I was born. I have reproduced the entries in the order in which they appear and without any omissions or redaction; only the names have been changed.

Excerpts from *Thy Neck with Chains of Gold* are from a play written by my mother in 1967. The suicide at the end of the play does not appear in the copy held by the Toronto Research Library, but was included in a 1969 performance in Montreal.

Comments on the article about the kibbutz boys were found on the internet.

John Snarey and Indiana University Press kindly allowed me to quote from Snarey's study of Kibbutz Sasa.

Articles attributed to the trade union newspaper *Davar* (now defunct) are authentic, as is the letter to the editor; translations are mine. Terrorists were commonly referred to at that time as "infiltrators." In the letter to the editor, only the title of the novel in question has been changed. I am grateful to the Lavon Institute of the New Histadrut for permission to reproduce these texts.

Naftali's unpublished war memoir was written by my father.

Professor Yuval Dror has generously allowed me to quote from his informative book, *The History of Kibbutz Education.*

Many thanks to Givat Haviva Jewish-Arab Centre for Peace for sending me Kibbutz Sasa's first Hagadda and allowing me to quote from it.

I am grateful to Maariv Newspapers for permission to reproduce Dimitri Berman's recollections of his trip to Petra.

I came across excerpts from Takhi's diary in *One Palestine, United*, Tom Segev's wonderful book about British-mandated Palestine (1923–1948). The diary was published in its entirety by Am Oved and edited by Yehuda Erez. I have fused and rearranged some of the entries.

The Israeli writer Rakefet Zohar graciously responded to my queries about the kibbutz *siḥa*, and allowed me to include her letter in my notes. I hope her important novel about teenagers on a kibbutz will be translated into English.